Heineken
WORLD
OF GOLF 95

Edited by Nick Edmund

Hodder & Stoughton

First published 1995

This edition produced for
Hodder & Stoughton
A division of Hodder Headline PLC
338 Euston Road
London NW1 3BH

Heineken World of Golf
Text © Nick Edmund
Photography © Allsport

Nick Edmund has asserted his right under
the Copyright, Designs and Patents Act, 1988
to be identified as the author of this work

A CIP catalogue record for this book is available
from the British Library
ISBN 0 340 64705 1

Assistant Editor Richard Dyson

Picture research by Andrew Redington
and Tim Matthews at Allsport

Designed by Rob Kelland at Allsport
Typeset in Gill and Joanna

Production by Mike Powell & Associates
Origination by Litho Origination Ltd, London
Printed by Butler & Tanner Ltd, England

.

PHOTOGRAPHIC CREDITS

David Cannon/Allsport: 5, 13 (both), 14 (all), 16, 17 (below), 18 (below), 19, 20 (right, below), 22-23, 27, 28-29, 30, 31, 32, 33, 42, 44 (both),
45, 49 (inset), 55 (left), 56, 57 (left, top), 58 (below), 74, 79 (below), 80 (below), 85, 86, 88 (inset), 88-89, 95 (below), 100, 109, 111, 112, 114, 115 (below),
116 (top), 117, 119 (inset), 126, 140, 143 (both), 147, 149, 153 (left), 155 (below), 168-169, 171 (below), 172 (right), 177 (both), 180 (left), 181 (both),
189 (below), 192, 194, 195 (both), 197, 199, 200, 207 (both), 212, 216-217, 218 (top), 219 (top, below), 220 (top, below right), 221 (all), 224;
Allsport: 26, 54, 58 (top), 103 (left), 116 (left, right), 164 (right), 165, 166, 176; **Simon Bruty/Allsport:** 18 (top), 20 (left), 62-63, 66, 67 (below, right),
68, 69, 71, 123, 133, 196, 206, 218 (below); **Chris Cole/Allsport:** 214; **Phil Cole/Allsport:** 78, 80 (top), 81 (top), 83, 84, 95 (left), 102, 179;
Michael Cooper/Allsport: 92 (centre), 118-119, 189 (left); **JD Cuban/Allsport USA:** 128, 129, 137, 183, 186, 187; **Stephen Dunn/Allsport USA:** 115 (above), 141;
Michael Hobbs/Allsport: 202; **Joe Mann/Allsport:** 155 (left); **Bob Martin/Allsport:** 203 (top); **Stephen Munday/Allsport:** 3, 8, 12, 20 (top), 24, 25, 39, 40, 41,
43 (below), 44 (top), 48-49, 53, 57 (below), 59, 76, 81 (below), 82, 90 (left, right), 91, 93 (below), 94, 95 (right), 96 (both), 97, 98, 99, 103 (right), 104, 105,
106, 107, 110, 113, 152 (left), 153 (right), 154, 155 (centre, right), 157, 158, 159 (both), 160 (both), 167, 170, 171 (top), 172 (left), 173 (both), 178,203 (below),
210, 211 (both), 213, 218-219, 220 (below, left); **Gary Newkirk Allsport/USA:** 15 (below), 17 (top), 36-37, 43 (top), 65, 70 (both), 120, 121, 122, 127, 130, 131,
136, 139, 142 (both), 144, 174-175, 188, 189 (right), 198, 222, 223 (below); **Gary M Prior/Allsport:** 10-11, 150-151, 152 (right), 208, 209 (right);
Andrew Redington/Allsport: 223 (top); **Dave Rogers/Allsport:** 50-51, 52, 55 (right), 180 (right), 209 (left); **Rick Stewart/Allsport USA:** 204, 205;
Anton Want/Allsport: 16 (inset), 93 (top), 162-163, 164 (left), 194 (both);
Nick Edmund: 6; **Bob Ewell:** 15 (top); **Phil Inglis:** 190 (all); **Rusty Jarrett:** 67 (top), 77, 79 (top), 182; **Debbie Newcombe:** 146; **Mark Newcombe:** 148, 185;

CONTENTS

4

GLOBAL GOLF

5

1995: A YEAR TO SAVOUR

6

GREAT GOLF COURSES OF THE WORLD

FOREWORD

by Fred Couples

It is my pleasure to welcome you to the 3rd edition of this beautifully produced *Heineken World of Golf* yearbook. I guess you only have to look at the back cover to see why I've been invited to contribute a Foreword!

Winning the Heineken World Cup in Puerto Rico last November was a special thrill for me, for many reasons. For one thing, it is always great fun to team-up with Davis – even when he booms it 20 yards past me, and, of course, it is always an honour to play for your country. There is also the tournament's unique atmosphere: it's serious business, for sure, but somehow the rivalry seems a little less tense and more friendly than at some other team events I can think of. To have won that giant cup three years in succession – at its 40th staging and with a score of 40 under par, we are really proud of that.

Last year was a bit of an up-and-down one for me. I began playing well at the start of '94, then became injured and lost my rhythm but fortunately I recovered my form towards the end of the season.

I've talked about me and the back cover of this book but it's the guys on the front cover who dominated. Ernie Els has had an incredible year and what can you say about Nick Price?

With its easy style and tremendous photography, this book tells the story of 1994 and whets the appetite for 1995. I must say I am really looking forward to the Major Championships next year: Augusta, Shinnecock Hills, St Andrews and Riviera – they're all great courses, and then there is the Ryder Cup and the Heineken World Cup in China to look forward to. I've never been to China; I hope Davis knows the way.

I'm sure you will enjoy reading this book and I hope you have a successful 1995, both on and off the fairways.

FRED COUPLES · *January 1995*

Go placidly amid the heather and the gorse and remember what peace there may be on the fairway. As far as possible without surrender be on good terms with all golfers. Remember to replace your divots and to repair your pitch marks; and listen to elder members, even the dull and ignorant; they all have their story. Avoid loud and aggressive caddies they are vexatious to the spirit.

If you compare your score with others you may become vain and bitter, for there will always be greater and lesser golfers than yourself. Enjoy your pars as well as your birdies. Keep interested in your handicap, however humble; it is a real possession in the changing fortunes of time. Exercise caution with your teeshots for the fairways may be riddled with hidden pot-bunkers. But let this not discourage you from swinging freely; many shots have found the green from thick rough and always there is the hope of a long putt.

Stay calm. Especially avoid losing your temper. Never be cynical about plus fours; for in the face of all aridity and disenchantment, they are as perennial as the tweaked three-footer. Take kindly the counsel of the years, gracefully surrendering the long drives of youth. Nurture strength from your short game to shield you in sudden misfortune. But do not distress yourself with imaginings. Many shots are wasted through fear of slicing and hooking.

With your Brassie, your Mashie and your favourite Niblick be content with yourself. You are a part of the links no less than the sandhills and the rabbit scrapes; you have a right to golf here. And whether or not it is clear to you, no doubt the golf links is unfolding as it should. Therefore be at peace with your game, whatever you conceive it to be and whatever the weather, come rain or shine, be at peace with your soul. With all its sham, drudgery and broken dreams, it is still a beautiful game. Be cheerful, strive to be happy.   N.E.E.

Discovered on a Gravestone
near Ballyliffin, Co. Donegal
Ireland c. 1750

INTRODUCTION

by Nick Edmund

The world is divided into two camps: those of us who have been bitten by the bug, and love golf and those who haven't and don't. Although we in the former camp believe those in the latter are deprived, there is still one retort that never fails to annoy us, 'Golf is a good walk spoiled'. We hope this book exposes the lie.

The *Heineken World of Golf* is a yearbook with a difference. It reviews the golfing season, describing the many great tournaments and the adventures of its myriad personalities but it also celebrates the international flavour of the sport, enjoying its rich geography as well as the immediate history.

Our 3rd edition comprises six chapters and it opens and closes with a burst of colour, courtesy of our award-winning photographers. In between, we explore the magic of the major championships and journey around all the significant tours of the world, charting golf in Europe, The United States, Australasia, Japan and South Africa. The book's content is not restricted to the men's professional season as women's golf, amateur golf, senior golf and international team golf are also given plenty of attention. As Fred Couples notes in his foreword, there is also a chapter where we bring out the crystal ball and look forward to 1995 – to a year that promises so much.

As editor of the *Heineken World of Golf*, I would like to express my sincere thanks to those people without whose support and encouragement this 3rd edition would never have materialised. I am grateful to all the contributing journalists for their fine commentaries, reports and previews, and to our aforementioned photographers, especially David Cannon of Allsport who is the book's principal photographer.

I'm sure you'll agree that this edition has been very attractively produced and much credit for this must go to the designer, Rob Kelland and to Mike Powell who has coordinated all the production work. It has also been put together remarkably quickly and, but for the help of Julie Kay, Andrew Redington and Tim Matthews at Allsport, half of the contents might still be on my dining room table – as well as scattered across the living room floor. A massive thank you also, then, to my wife Teresa. Finally, of course, a big thank you to our publishers and to our generous sponsor, Heineken.

Cheers to all of them… and best wishes to you. Go placidly in '95!

NICK EDMUND · *January 1995*

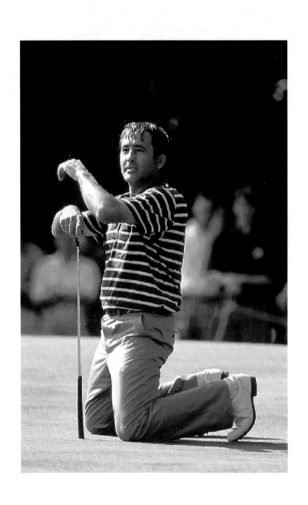

1994
A YEAR TO REMEMBER

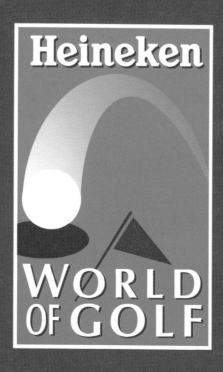

1994
A YEAR TO REMEMBER

From the Pacific to the Atlantic: while Arnold Palmer (previous pages)
pondered at Pebble Beach, Jack Nicklaus and friends posed at Turnberry.
Nicklaus and Watson fought our their famous 'Duel in Sun' at Turnberry in 1977;
prior to the start of the 1994 Open they challenged Nick Price and Greg Norman
(the 1986 winner at Turnberry) to a friendly fourball. Apparently the 'youngsters'
got a thrashing – but by the end of the week Price was the Open champion

Through the
mist and
despite the heat
they emerged
in 1994.
(Above)
Ernie Els and
José-Maria
Olazabal
realised their
potential and
gained their
first major
championship
victories

Colin
Montgomerie
didn't win
a Major –
although he
came close at
Oakmont – but
he climbed into
the top 10 of
the world
rankings and
emphatically
retained his
European Order
of Merit crown

What is Japanese for annus mirabilis?
Masashi 'Jumbo' Ozaki was even more dominant
in Japan than Nick Price was in America
and Colin Montgomerie in Europe. He won seven
tournaments, including the Japan Open by 13 strokes
and the Daiwa International by 15. It wasn't just
his fellow countrymen whom he beat for when
the 'rest of the world' took him on in November's
Taiheiyo Masters and Dunlop Phoenix events,
Jumbo triumphed on both occasions – winning
the former by five shots and the latter with
a birdie at the final hole for a
closing round of 65

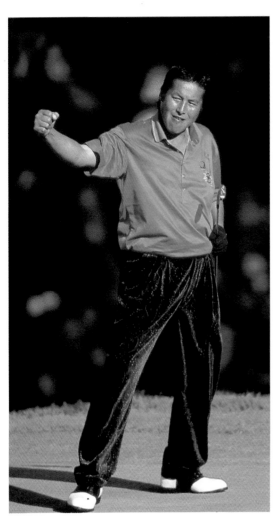

(Top left) High Noon became high fives at The Greenbrier when America's women stormed to victory in October's Solheim Cup. (Centre left) Canada was the surprise winner of the Alfred Dunhill Cup, defeating the US in the final at St Andrews. (Below left) Fred Couples and Davis Love created history by claiming the Heineken World Cup in Puerto Rico for the third year in succession. Now for China in '95?

The biggest hitter in women's golf became its greatest player in 1994. Not only did Laura Davies top the LPGA Money List in America (and win a Major) but she became the first ever golfer – male or female – to win tournaments on five different Tours during the same calendar year. 'Long' John Daly also made headlines in 1994 (when doesn't he make headlines?) but not always for the right reasons

(Main picture)
Ernie Els,
'the next
dominant
player' was on
the beach at
St Andrews
in 1994 –
practising
for next
year's Open
Championship
perhaps?

Two months
after Els' win in
the US Open,
another
potential
superstar,
18 year old
Eldrick 'Tiger'
Woods (inset)
won the
US Amateur.
Els versus
Woods at
St Andrews
in the
year 2000?

(Above) What a way to finish the year!
Mark McCumber holed a huge birdie
putt to defeat Fuzzy Zoeller in a
play-off for the US PGA Tour's
season-ending Tour Championship.
From A to Z: we began this pictorial
review with Arnold Palmer in reflective
mood at Pebble Beach and a famous
quartet posing at Turnberry;
how's this for a reflective pose,
courtesy of the cool Mr Zoeller

A tale of
two Nicks:
Nick Faldo
began the year
as the world's
number one
but by the end
of December
Nick Price
was on top

WORLD RANKINGS

31ST · DECEMBER · 1994

SONY RANKINGS

POSITION PLAYER	CIRCUIT	POINTS
1 Nick Price	Afr	21.19
2 Greg Norman	ANZ	20.57
3 Nick Faldo	Eur	16.93
4 Bernhard Langer	Eur	15.32
5 José-Maria Olazabal	Eur	15.18
6 Ernie Els	Afr	14.70
7 Fred Couples	USA	12.86
8 Colin Montgomerie	Eur	12.19
9 Masashi Ozaki	Jpn	11.39
10 Corey Pavin	USA	10.87
11 David Frost	Afr	9.88
12 Fuzzy Zoeller	USA	9.73
13 Tom Kite	USA	9.03
14 Seve Ballesteros	Eur	8.96
15 Vijay Singh	Asa	8.49
16 Ian Woosnam	Eur	8.46
17 Tom Lehman	USA	8.13
18 Mark McNulty	Afr	8.01
19 Mark McCumber	USA	7.68
20 Loren Roberts	USA	7.46
21 Paul Azinger	USA	7.25
22 Phil Mickelson	USA	7.24
23 Tom Watson	USA	6.82
24 John Cook	USA	6.67
25 Davis Love III	USA	6.53
26 Brad Faxon	USA	6.43
27 Jeff Maggert	USA	6.20
28 Larry Mize	USA	6.14
29 Hale Irwin	USA	5.96
30 Scott Hoch	USA	5.91
31 Frank Nobilo	ANZ	5.74
32 Lee Janzen	USA	5.68
33 David Gilford	Eur	5.59
34 Ben Crenshaw	USA	5.58
35 Barry Lane	Eur	5.48
36 Bill Glasson	USA	5.47
37 Bob Estes	USA	5.36
38 Sam Torrance	Eur	5.23
39 Jesper Parnevik	Eur	5.23
40 John Huston	USA	5.22
41 Bruce Lietzke	USA	5.22
42 Miguel A Jimenez	Eur	5.20
43 Steve Elkington	ANZ	5.18
44 Craig Parry	ANZ	5.14
45 David Edwards	USA	5.07
46 Tsun'ki Nakajima	Jpn	5.00
47 Jay Haas	USA	4.99
48 Robert Allenby	ANZ	4.94
49 Mark Calcavecchia	USA	4.92
50 Rick Fehr	USA	4.82
51 Mark Roe	Eur	4.68
52 Eduardo Romero	SAm	4.67
53 Peter Senior	ANZ	4.60
54 Payne Stewart	USA	4.59
55 Mark James	Eur	4.54
56 Joakim Haeggman	Eur	4.42
57 Scott Simpson	USA	4.41
58 Curtis Strange	USA	4.33
59 Craig Stadler	USA	4.32
60 Gordon Brand Jnr	Eur	4.30

PING LEADERBOARD

POSITION PLAYER	COUNTRY	POINTS
1 Laura Davies	Eng	338.32
2 Liselotte Neumann	Swe	216.65
3 Beth Daniel	US	189.58
4 Donna Andrews	US	176.42
5 Betsy King	US	175.05
6 Dottie Mochrie	US	171.45
7 Helen Alfredsson	Swe	164.55
8 Patty Sheehan	US	160.17
9 Tammie Green	US	157.98
10 Brandie Burton	US	125.88
11 Jane Geddes	US	121.53
12 Meg Mallon	US	119.53
13 Kelly Robbins	US	118.78
14 Mayumi Hirase	Jap	114.05
15 Sherri Steinhauer	US	113.91
16 Elaine Crosby	US	103.70
17 Hiromi Kobayashi	Jap	99.09
18 Lauri Merten	US	96.78
19 Michelle McGann	US	93.21
20 Deb Richard	US	92.05
21 Jae-Sook Won	Kor	89.60
22 Dawn Coe-Jones	Can	89.40
23 Ayako Okamoto	Jap	84.18
24 Michiko Hattori	Jap	84.13
25 Annika Sorenstam	Swe	77.38
26 Pat Bradley	US	76.99
27 Ikuyo Shiotani	Jap	76.20
28 Trish Johnson	Eng	76.02
29 Judy Dickinson	US	75.69
30 Val Skinner	US	74.65

Laura Davies

2

THE MAJORS

THE MASTERS

THE US OPEN

THE OPEN CHAMPIONSHIP

THE USPGA

Heineken

WORLD
OF GOLF

THE MASTERS

THE MASTERS

ROLL · OF · HONOUR

1934		Horton Smith
1935	*	Gene Sarazen
1936		Horton Smith
1937		Byron Nelson
1938		Henry Picard
1939		Ralph Guldahl
1940		Jimmy Demaret
1941		Craig Wood
1942	*	Byron Nelson
1943-5		No championships played
1946		Herman Keiser
1947		Jimmy Demaret
1948		Claude Harmon
1949		Sam Snead
1950		Jimmy Demaret
1951		Ben Hogan
1952		Sam Snead
1953		Ben Hogan
1954	*	Sam Snead
1955		Cary Middlecoff
1956		Jack Burke
1957		Doug Ford
1958		Arnold Palmer
1959		Art Wall
1960		Arnold Palmer
1961		Gary Player
1962	*	Arnold Palmer
1963		Jack Nicklaus
1964		Arnold Palmer
1965		Jack Nicklaus
1966	*	Jack Nicklaus
1967		Gay Brewer
1968		Bob Goalby
1969		George Archer

1970	*	Billy Casper
1971		Charles Coody
1972		Jack Nicklaus
1973		Tommy Aaron
1974		Gary Player
1975		Jack Nicklaus
1976		Ray Floyd
1977		Tom Watson
1978		Gary Player
1979	*	Fuzzy Zoeller
1980		Seve Ballesteros
1981		Tom Watson
1982	*	Craig Stadler
1983		Seve Ballesteros
1984		Ben Crenshaw
1985		Bernhard Langer
1986		Jack Nicklaus
1987	*	Larry Mize
1988		Sandy Lyle
1989	*	Nick Faldo
1990	*	Nick Faldo
1991		Ian Woosnam
1992		Fred Couples
1993		Bernhard Langer
1994		José-Maria Olazabal

* Winner in play-off.

Ben Crenshaw, winner of the 1984 Masters

· HIGHLIGHTS ·

MOST WINS:
6 Jack Nicklaus
4 Arnold Palmer

MOST TIMES RUNNER-UP:
4 Ben Hogan
Tom Weiskopf
Jack Nicklaus

BIGGEST MARGIN OF VICTORY:
9 Jack Nicklaus (1965)

LOWEST WINNING TOTAL:
271 Jack Nicklaus (1965)
Ray Floyd (1976)

LOWEST SINGLE ROUND:
63 Nick Price (1986)

RECORD FRONT NINE:
30 Johnny Miller (1975)
Greg Norman (1988)

RECORD BACK NINE:
29 Mark Calcavecchia (1992)

LOWEST FINAL ROUND BY WINNER:
64 Gary Player (1978)

OLDEST CHAMPION:
Jack Nicklaus,
aged 46 (1986)

YOUNGEST CHAMPION:
Severiano Ballesteros,
aged 23 (1980)

THE 1994 MASTERS

Augusta: 'where the golf world goes to see the beauty;
to know the peril, to look for ghosts and to listen for echoes'

Ron Green, Charlotte Observer

The British Open, July 1979: a different continent, a generation ago... remember Royal Lytham? It was the occasion when Seve Ballesteros fulfilled his *destino*. On the eve of the final round of that championship, Roberto de Vicenzo, the Argentinian elder statesman who had taken the young Spaniard under his wing, offered his advice, 'Tienes las manos, Ahora juega con tu corazon' – you have the hands, now play with your heart. And of course the next day Seve went out and played with his heart.

The final round of The Masters, April 1994: another day, another destiny. Lying in second place, just a stroke behind Tom Lehman, José-Maria Olazabal arrives at the course to discover that a note has been left in his locker. Roughly translated from the Spanish it reads: 'Go there, be patient. Allow the others to become nervous. Play your own game. You know what you have to do – you are the best player in the world. Good Luck.' In 1979 de Vicenzo had urged Ballesteros to play with his heart; now Seve was telling Olazabal to play with his head.

But what business did Olazabal – runner-up to Ian Woosnam in 1991 – have in winning the 1994 Masters anyway? An opening 74, which left him six strokes behind first round leader Larry Mize, was hardly the stuff of champions and in any case, surely this was the

An artist at work: Seve Ballesteros at Augusta

year when Greg Norman would finally claim that elusive first Green Jacket?

Norman's form going into the Masters appeared irresistible. Just a fortnight earlier he had won the Players Championship with an astonishing score of 24 under par and with a performance described by Ray Floyd as, 'The best golf played anywhere in the world, maybe ever.' Could Norman transport his Midas Touch from Florida to Georgia? Is there anything

With a stiff breeze adding to the confusion, only three players, Mize, Tom Kite and Fulton Allem broke 70 and the average score that day was 74.7.

The par five 15th proved to be the principal card wrecker with players finding it almost impossible to hold their approach shots on the green. It wasn't just a case of sixes and sevens, though, there were eights and nines, and even one ten. Norman was one of many who

The 1987 champion, Larry Mize set the early pace. (Opposite page) Augusta's glorious 10th – where traditionally The Masters 'begins' on Sunday

more tantalisingly fickle than form?

While the Australian wondered and hoped as the tournament got underway, much of the field was tearing its hair out in frustration. Augusta looked magnificent – perhaps even more beautiful than usual this Spring – but the golf course had been mischievously prepared, with ultra-slick, ultra-firm greens and, on Thursday at least, several horrid pin placements.

watched in disbelief as his second shot spun back off the putting surface and into Rae's Creek. Tom Watson's fate was even worse. He chipped, seemingly so deftly, from behind the flag yet saw his ball gather momentum as it raced across the green, refusing to stop until it trickled off down the bank into the water. Watson's nightmare probably cost him the first day lead, for although he took an eight at the

15th he still managed to score a 70. Norman, whose round resembled the proverbial rollercoaster – it comprised six bogeys, five pars, six birdies and one eagle, also returned a 70. Several 'big names' struggled, however: Nick Price, the second favourite, took 74, as did the defending champion, Bernhard Langer and, as mentioned, Olazabal. Nick Faldo and Ian Woosnam both shot 76.

There were far fewer tales of woe on Friday, a day when, to be frank, not a great deal of note happened. Larry Mize composed a 71 for a five under par 36-hole total of 139 and remained one ahead of the field. Norman occasionally threatened to catch fire but never really succeeded – still, a second successive round of 70 kept him very much in the thick of things. The two Toms, Watson and Kite, remained there or thereabouts and although Messrs Price, Langer, Faldo and Woosnam all survived the halfway cut, they were still a long way down the leaderboard. The most significant move on Friday was made by Olazabal, whose five under par 67 advanced him to within two strokes of the lead.

So Augusta-born Larry Mize was still leading the Masters (not a good omen for Norman) and with Fred Couples, Paul Azinger and Phil Mickelson all absent through injury, American hopes for a home victory rested largely with the 1987 champion and the two Toms, both now well into their 40s. The two Toms? Better make that the three Toms.

Like Norman, 35 year old Tom Lehman had begun 70-70, but nothwithstanding his joint third place finish in 1993 (in his first Masters appearance) few believed he would play a prominent role come the weekend. The reason was simple enough: he had never won a

Greg Norman and his caddie look to the heavens. If the Shark was hoping for divine inspiration, none seemed to come his way

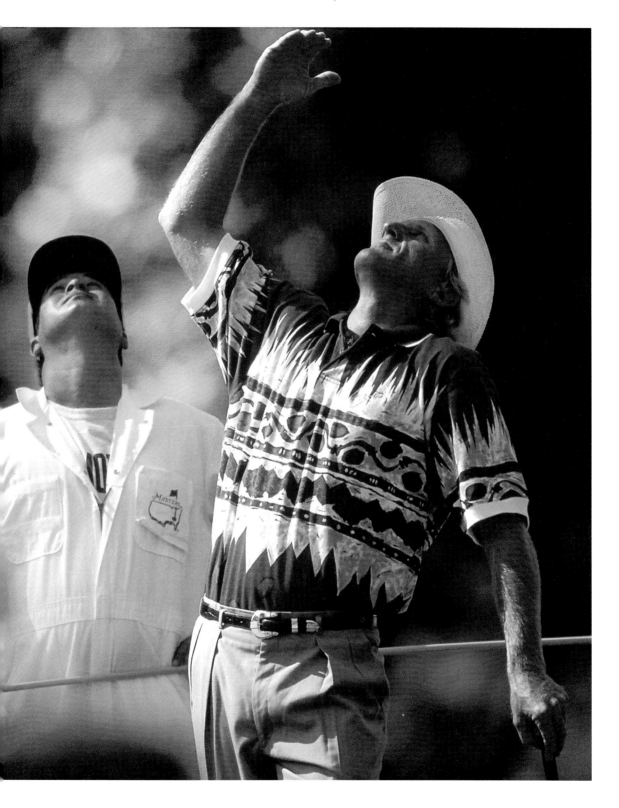

regular US tournament, never mind a major championship. The well-travelled Lehman was, according to the Augusta Chronicle, 'A veteran of more Tours than the Rolling Stones'.

On Masters Saturday Greg Norman didn't so much ignite as implode. The man who was meant to win the Masters shot a birdie-free 75 and plummeted down the leaderboard. Once again the Australian's Green Jacket was put back into mothballs. With Watson and Kite suffering

the 12th) it was Lehman and Olazabal who were playing the superior golf. Mize's solid 72 was made to look ordinary by the 69s of his two closest pursuers. The Spaniard 'peppered the flagsticks' throughout the day while the highlight of Lehman's round was an amazing 50 foot birdie putt at the 16th. After 54 holes it was Lehman who now led on 209, by one from Olazabal (210) and by two from Mize (211).

A bank of azaleas provides a striking backdrop as Olazabal contemplates his approach to the 13th in the final round

on the greens, mid way through the third round the 58th Masters appeared to be shaping into a three way contest between Mize, Olazabal and Lehman.

If Mize was the one holing all the eight-footers (in addition to a spectacular bunker shot at

'Be patient... Play your own game', Ballesteros urged his compatriot. Olazabal set about doing precisely that in Sunday's final round. This time Mize had no miracles up his sleeve and although he challenged strongly in the early part of his round a succession of missed putts on the back nine effectively dashed his hopes. Now there were just two – Olazabal and Lehman.

**Sheer agony
for Tom Lehman
as his putt for
an eagle at the
15th refuses
to drop**

The closing moments of the 1994 Masters: Olazabal chips to the flag at the 72nd hole

It was a little reminiscent of the 1993 Masters, when the closing holes developed into a duel between Bernhard Langer and Chip Beck: a European versus an American. Then, it was the German's eagle at the 13th that decided the issue; 12 months later it was to be a Spanish eagle at the 15th. But whereas Beck failed to raise his game and chase Langer, Lehman did everything in his power to match the Spaniard's brilliance. His own eagle attempt at the 15th (he trailed Olazabal by a single stroke after 14 holes and had hit his approach much closer) slid agonisingly past the cup. And there was more drama on the 16th and 17th when the American narrowly missed birdie putts from six feet and 12 feet. Olazabal's only blemish was to take three putts at the 17th but he was still one ahead as he walked to the 18th tee.

Destino awaited. Fate and the 72nd hole of the Masters – so cruel to Olazabal three years earlier – now smiled upon the young Spaniard. With Lehman stumbling to a bogey five, an adventurous, up-and-down par four proved more than sufficient. German steel had been followed by Spanish gold.

Now, as with Ballesteros in 1979, the golfing world is his oyster. And the Spanish Succession is complete.

1994 MASTERS

FINAL · SCORES

No more the Young Pretender. Bernhard Langer welcomes Olazabal to the most exclusive club in golf

J M Olazabal	74	67	69	69	279	$360,000	B Langer	74	74	72	73	293	16,800
T Lehman	70	70	69	72	281	216,000	J Sluman	74	75	71	73	293	16,800
L Mize	68	71	72	71	282	136,000	S Simpson	74	74	73	73	294	14,800
T Kite	69	72	71	71	283	96,000	V Singh	70	75	74	75	294	14,800
J Haas	72	72	72	69	285	73,000	C Strange	74	70	75	75	294	14,800
J McGovern	72	70	71	72	285	73,000	L Janzen	75	71	76	73	295	13,300
L Roberts	75	68	72	70	285	73,000	C Parry	75	74	73	73	295	13,300
E Els	74	67	74	71	286	60,000	N Faldo	76	73	73	74	296	12,400
C Pavin	71	72	73	70	286	60,000	R Cochran	71	74	74	78	297	11,500
I Baker-Finch	71	71	71	74	287	50,000	S Torrance	76	73	74	74	297	11,500
R Floyd	70	74	71	72	287	50,000	D Frost	74	71	75	78	298	10,300
J Huston	72	72	74	69	287	50,000	N Price	74	73	74	77	298	10,300
T Watson	70	71	73	74	288	42,000	F Zoeller	74	72	74	78	298	10,300
D Forsman	74	66	76	73	289	38,000	F Allem	69	77	76	77	299	9,000
C Beck	71	71	75	74	291	34,000	F Funk	79	70	75	75	299	9,000
B Faxon	71	73	73	74	291	34,000	S Lyle	75	73	78	73	299	9,000
M O'Meara	75	70	76	70	291	34,000	W Grady	74	73	73	80	300	7,400
S Ballesteros	70	76	75	71	292	24,343	A Magee	74	74	76	76	300	7,400
B Crenshaw	74	73	73	72	292	24,343	H Meshiai	71	71	80	78	300	7,400
D Edwards	73	72	73	74	292	24,343	C Rocca	79	70	78	73	300	7,400
B Glasson	72	73	75	72	292	24,343	M Standly	77	69	79	75	300	7,400
H Irwin	73	68	79	72	292	24,343	J Cook	77	72	77	75	301	6,000
G Norman	70	70	75	77	292	24,343	I Woosnam	76	73	77	75	301	6,000
L Wadkins	73	74	73	72	292	24,343	J Daly	76	73	77	78	304	5,250

THE MASTERS: THE GREAT AMERICAN MYSTERY

A Commentary by Derek Lawrenson

In Europe, the late-night television pictures of the Masters have habitually encouraged people to root out the golf clubs from wherever they may have been hidden. Meanwhile, in the host country, the event has introduced a new rite of spring: what's wrong with American golf?

Come April, and seemingly everyone is bursting forth with answers to this question. They begin by wailing: what the hell's going on? If it's not Sandy Lyle from Shrewsbury, Scotland, winning, it's Iron Woosnam from Oswestry, Wales. Then there's Bernhard Longer or Steve Ballesteros. In 1994 there came another who has absolutely no chance of having everything pronounced properly since his name alone contains nine syllables – not to mention a hyphen.

But let's turn the question around a little: why have Europeans been measured up for six of the last seven green jackets on offer? Is it the absence of a collar of rough around the Augusta greens, as is normally to be found on US tour pit stops? Or the lack of rough full stop, perhaps?

These are undoubtedly important factors. But for all the criticism of The Masters, from the ludicrous charge that the course is non-American in character to the controversial policy of inviting just 80 or so players, the fact remains that the tournament has done a masterful job of identifying the best player in the world as its winner.

Lyle was the best in 1988. Faldo was number one in 1989 and 1990. Would you have favoured anyone over Ian Woosnam in 1991? And in 1992 it was only right that an American should enjoy a rare success for

Freddie Couples was untouchable for much of that year.

Severiano Ballesteros said to anyone who was prepared to listen at the 1993 Ryder Cup that José-Maria Olazabal was now the best golfer in the world. Supporters of Ernie Els and, in particular, Nick Price, could now, of course, put together a good case to counter that argument but few would surely disagree that Augusta '94 produced another winner of the very highest calibre.

Here we meet head-on this 'what's wrong with American golf' nonsense. Nothing's wrong. Why accentuate a negative? Why not acknowledge that just for once the best golfers produced in this particular generation have come largely from Europe? To argue any other way is simply to deny them the credit that's due. Not that such a thing will stop the American inquisition.

Where better to flourish than at The Masters? At Augusta, where the greatest golfer of all, Jack Nicklaus, enjoyed so many of his finest moments; where Arnold Palmer produced some of his most famous charges. At Augusta, where there is no rough to speak of (because the architect didn't want to take the driver out of a player's hands and didn't want to discourage power and an adventuresome spirit) but where a bad drive will leave a player badly positioned and a really bad drive will leave him behind a tree. Where there is no collar of rough around the greens because that detracts from the flair and the imagination of the short game experts. Have rough and every player becomes the same because they've all got to use an identical 'flop' shot to get out. Have none but make the greens full of slopes and subtle breaks and hollows and now there is a test of skill.

In 1991, Olazabal was ready for this test with regard to golfing expertise and courage but not in terms of the experience of coping with such an exacting occasion as being in contention over the closing stages.

One hole to go and a par four on the uphill final hole would have matched Woosnam's eventual winning score. Olazabal, stumbling from bunker to bunker, took five. Rarely has a bogey been more hurtfully received. To such an intense character, who had been told from the age of 20 that he would win majors, and win them soon, to fail so glaringly at the age of 25 was a bitter loss.

It's fair to say that Olazabal was not a barrel of laughs for a couple of seasons thereafter. Hitherto he could be charming and humorous: there was no better moment, for example, at Europe's historic 1987 Ryder Cup victory in America than when Olazabal indulged in an impromptu conga on the final green. Now he was just sullen.

For the first time a question mark had appeared against his golfing reputation. What once had appeared so certain was now not so certain at all. People began to doubt his technique. How can a swing so quick possibly withstand the pressure of being in contention playing the 18th hole? The fact that Olazabal rarely sought advice exacerbated the situation.

But didn't this fast swing withstand all the pressure that two Ryder Cups could produce? That was conveniently forgotten. Everything was now forgotten amidst the indelible image of taking a bogey five where nothing worse than a par four had been permitted.

Faldo took three years out of his golfing life to come up with a solution to such a problem, opting for major swing surgery. In a way, Olazabal took three years as well.

The difference was that he chose to refine rather than rebuild. He stuck with what he had and worked instead on his attitude. It was a good decision for boy, was there work to do.

Perfectionism is an unhappy trait in a golfer. The very nature of the game means that no-one can be perfect any of the time let alone all. A perfect round would mean holing every iron approach to the green and a round of 36. As the illusionist's dream of perfection revealed itself so Olazabal's dark side took over and his golf went out of the window.

Olazabal vowed to change for the 1994 campaign. For the first time since he was a teenager he played some social golf during the close season and learned afresh the joys of the game when played simply for pleasure.

As therapy this worked wonders. Olazabal played five tournaments leading up to Augusta. He won one, finished second twice, and came ninth and 14th in the other two.

In the third round at The Masters there were a couple of examples of this change of resolve when Olazabal's shots to the 14th and 15th greens, both bang on line, finished 35ft behind the flag each time. One would have been hard to bear in days gone by. Two would have provoked, at best, a terrible rant at his caddie. On each occasion Olazabal just shrugged.

What happened on the final day, then, was triumphant vindication of the road he had chosen to pursue, to concentrate on the mind rather than the swing. Olazabal shot 69 in that final round, the joint best score of the day. There was no error-strewn bogey on the last hole this time. That belonged to the gallant runner-up, Tom Lehman, who came into the media room straight after his round. His hands were busy. One greeted the chairman of the Masters Press Committee, Charlie Yates. The other held on to his four year old daughter, Rachel. 'Questions?' Yates asked.

'Yeh Tom', a man with a Southern accent drawled. 'What's wrong with American golf?'

THE US OPEN

THE US OPEN

ROLL · OF · HONOUR

1895	Horace Rawlins	1938	Ralph Guldahl	1983	Larry Nelson
1896	James Foulis	1939	* Byron Nelson	1984	* Fuzzy Zoeller
1897	Joe Lloyd	1940	* Lawson Little	1985	Andy North
1898	Fred Herd	1941	Craig Wood	1986	Ray Floyd
1899	Willie Smith	1942-5	No championships played	1987	Scott Simpson
1900	Harry Vardon	1946	* Lloyd Mangrum	1988	* Curtis Strange
1901	* Willie Anderson	1947	* Lew Worsham	1989	Curtis Strange
1902	Laurie Auchterlonie	1948	Ben Hogan	1990	* Hale Irwin
1903	* Willie Anderson	1949	Cary Middlecoff	1991	* Payne Stewart
1904	Willie Anderson	1950	* Ben Hogan	1992	Tom Kite
1905	Willie Anderson	1951	Ben Hogan	1993	Lee Janzen
1906	Alex Smith	1952	Julius Boros	1994	* Ernie Els
1907	Alex Ross	1953	Ben Hogan		
1908	* Fred McLeod	1954	Ed Furgol		
1909	George Sargent	1955	* Jack Fleck		
1910	* Alex Smith	1956	Cary Middlecoff		
1911	* John McDermott	1957	* Dick Mayer		
1912	John McDermott	1958	Tommy Bolt		
1913	* Francis Ouimet	1959	Billy Casper		
1914	Walter Hagen	1960	Arnold Palmer		
1915	Jerome Travers	1961	Gene Littler		
1916	Charles Evans, Jr	1962	* Jack Nicklaus		
1917-18	No championships played	1963	* Julius Boros		
1919	* Walter Hagen	1964	Ken Venturi		
1920	Edward Ray	1965	* Gary Player		
1921	James M. Barnes	1966	* Billy Casper		
1922	Gene Sarazen	1967	Jack Nicklaus		
1923	* Robert T. Jones	1968	Lee Trevino		
1924	Cyril Walker	1969	Orville Moody		
1925	* W. MacFarlane	1970	Tony Jacklin		
1926	Robert T. Jones	1971	* Lee Trevino		
1927	* Tommy Armour	1972	Jack Nicklaus		
1928	* Johnny Farrell	1973	Johnny Miller		
1929	Robert T. Jones	1974	Hale Irwin		
1930	Robert T. Jones	1975	* Lou Graham		
1931	* Billy Burke	1976	Jerry Pate		
1932	Gene Sarazen	1977	Hubert Green		
1933	Johnny Goodman	1978	Andy North		
1934	Olin Dutra	1979	Hale Irwin		
1935	Sam Parks, Jr	1980	Jack Nicklaus		
1936	Tony Manero	1981	David Graham		
1937	Ralph Guldahl	1982	Tom Watson		

* Winner in play-off.

· HIGHLIGHTS ·

MOST WINS:
4 Willie Anderson
Bobby Jones
Ben Hogan
Jack Nicklaus

MOST TIMES RUNNER-UP:
4 Bobby Jones
Sam Snead
Arnold Palmer
Jack Nicklaus

BIGGEST MARGIN OF VICTORY:
9 Willie Smith (1899)
Jim Barnes (1921)

LOWEST WINNING TOTAL:
272 Jack Nicklaus (1980)
Lee Janzen (1993)

LOWEST SINGLE ROUND:
63 Johnny Miller (1973)
Tom Weiskopf (1980)
Jack Nicklaus (1980)

LOWEST FINAL ROUND BY WINNER:
63 Johnny Miller (1973)

OLDEST CHAMPION:
Hale Irwin, aged 45 (1990)

YOUNGEST CHAMPION:
Johnny McDermott,
aged 19 (1911)

THE 1994 US OPEN

The 94th US Open was a watershed championship:
at Oakmont, in sauna-like conditions, all our yesterdays
met with all our tomorrows

The temperature was in the high 90s but Arnie's army were out in force cheering every move he made. Jack Nicklaus crouched over a 40 foot putt to take the lead in the championship as Johnny Miller, his playing partner, looked on. Tom Watson was getting ready to play a superlative round of golf that would eclipse even Nicklaus' performance. It had to be the US Open. It had to be Oakmont.

Situated on the outskirts of Pittsburgh, Oakmont is one of America's greatest and most historic courses. By general consent, the three greatest golfers of all time have been Bobby Jones, Ben Hogan and Jack Nicklaus: each won a National Championship at Oakmont – the only course that can make such a claim. Two other golfing legends, Gene Sarazen and Sam Snead won USPGA Championships here. Oakmont is where, in 1962, Nicklaus defeated Arnold Palmer in a play-off to win his first major and where eleven years later, Johnny Miller produced the finest closing round in championship history.

Yet Oakmont is hard to love. It is no beauty. 'Oakmont', Sarazen once said, 'has all the charm of a sock to the head.' It also been described as 'an 18-headed hydra; Hades on Hulton Road.' Certainly, its 1st and 18th holes are both monsters. Oakmont is the ultimate

1962 revisited: Jack Nicklaus rolls back the years

monument to the penal school of golf architecture. Its fairway bunkering is prodigious; it is at Oakmont, of course, where the notorious Church Pew bunker is found.

Greatness, history and challenge: now throw in the weather. 'Blazing June' – it was a month of record temperatures across America. Pittsburgh steamed; Oakmont sweltered and the players found it mightily oppressive.

It was in such conditions that 54 year old

Colin Montgomerie suffered more than most in the conditions, yet still produced the finest championship performance of his career

Jack Nicklaus decided to turn back the clock – by all of 32 years. 'I am not surprised... I am amazed', said Nicklaus when he holed his 40 footer at the last for a 69. Johnny Miller was

neither surprised nor amazed as he had seen it all before. Tom Watson, no 'spring chicken' himself at 44, was the only player who bettered Nicklaus' score. 'When I saw Jack's name up there I thought, there's no reason why Watson cannot do it as well. It inspired me.' Watson, as he had done for much of the time at Augusta (and would later do at Turnberry) struck the ball beautifully in his round of 68. Three-time champion Hale Irwin and two of the ever-increasing overseas contingent, South African Ernie Els and New Zealand's Frank Nobilo matched Nicklaus' 69.

Colin Montgomerie produced the best European performance in the opening round. At one stage he stood three under par for the championship but dropped three strokes in a poor finish. The heat affected him: 'my hands swelled up and felt like sausages', he said. Scotland must have seemed a world away.

Guess who led the US Open after two rounds on Friday evening? 'Blue skies, 65', Greg Norman allegedly repeats to himself when he awakens with that special feeling that 'today's going to be his day'. Well, 'today' wasn't his day – the Great White Shark added a workmanlike 71 to go with his opening 71 – 'today' was the 'Pink Lobster's' day... good old Monty. Notwithstanding the heat, which somehow seemed to bypass his straw hat and redden his features, he was the player who scored a dazzling 65. Montgomerie had an eagle and five birdies in his round and, unlike the previous day, he finished in style with a three at the last. Montgomerie's 65 catapulted him to the head of the field and after 36 holes he held a two shot lead over Irwin and John Cook. There was never a prospect, however, of his enjoying principal headline status in all the world's newspapers the following morning, for Friday was the occasion of Arnold Palmer's final round in the US Open. It mattered not a jot, of course, that Palmer bogeyed his final hole and easily missed the cut. He received a standing ovation throughout the entire length of the 18th hole and there were tears in his eyes when he left the green. John Hopkins described it neatly in the *The Times*: 'He waved that massive white paw of his, hitched up his trousers and was gone.'

Jack Nicklaus may also be close to his final US Open curtain call, but if this was to be his last championship at Oakmont he was clearly

early. 'Since the 1993 US Open,' Larry Dormann commented wryly, 'the only thing that has gone up as much as Janzen's stroke average has been his bank balance.'

What might be termed, 'the Southern Hemisphere challenge' was not being led, as expected, by Norman and Price, but by Els and Nobilo. For two days they had returned identical scores of 69-71 to be handily placed on the 140 mark. After three rounds they were,

New Zealand's Frank Nobilo was a major contender for 54 holes

signing off in style. Nicklaus ended the day in joint 4th position, just three behind Montgomerie and his score of 70 might have been one or two strokes better, as had seemed likely when he birdied two of the first five holes.

While Montgomerie was busy composing the round of his life, his more famous Ryder Cup partner was busy missing the cut. Nick Faldo failed to avoid the halfway axe for the first time in a major championship since the 1986 USPGA – in the days before he remodelled his swing. At least Faldo was in distinguished company though for, in addition to Palmer, more surprisingly, both Nick Price and José Maria Olazabal (who would share the season's other three majors) joined him. The defending champion, Lee Janzen, also departed

respectively, first and second, Els producing a superb 66 on Saturday and Nobilo a fine 68.

By contrast it was all a bit of a struggle for Montgomerie. His 73 was hardly ruinous but his greatest asset, his usually arrow-straight driving, deserted him in the third round.

The platform for Els' 66 was established in the first five holes. He played them remarkably, scoring birdie-birdie-par-eagle-birdie – five under par. At the 9th he narrowly missed a putt for his second eagle to be out in 30. Momentum was lost, somewhat, when Els double-bogeyed the difficult 10th, although he finished with two birdies to establish a two stroke lead.

A few of the more parochial, or less informed members among the American

Ernie Els plays from one of Oakmont's myriad fairway bunkers

galleries wondered, 'Ernie Who?' At 24 years of age the young 'Star of Africa' was already an international force (see Tim Rosaforte's Commentary ahead)... now he was about to become a star in America.

A second great round was played on Saturday – a day when only nine players scored under 70 – and that came from Loren Roberts. Roberts, a quiet Californian, bettered Els' score by two strokes (not to mention his own first round 76 by twelve) due largely to his taking only 24 putts. 'I am a methodical, monotonous kind of golfer', he declared. In other words, Roberts is the archetypal US Open type player: a Scott Simpson-Curtis Strange type golfer. Remember Strange? The winnner in 1988 and 1989 (and who has done precious little of note since), was back on the leaderboard at Oakmont. Methodical, monotonous rounds of 70-70-70 did the trick for Strange. That other archetypal US Open golfer, Hale Irwin, now aged 49, was also lurking near the top of the leaderboard after 54 holes. Sadly, Nicklaus stopped turning back the clock on Saturday, shooting a 77, but his old sparring partner, Watson bounced back with his second 68 of the championship, a score bettered only by Els and Roberts. So, on Saturday evening, Els led on 206 (7 under par), then came Nobilo on 208, Montgomerie, Roberts, Irwin and Watson on 209 and Strange on 210.

It has been suggested that one of the chief differences between a US Open and a British Open is that whereas someone usually 'wins' the British Open (witness Nick Price's final three holes at Turnberry) the US Open is frequently 'lost'. Like, in a heavyweight championship boxing match, the player who wins is the one who has survived the longest. This may be a generalisation, and an unfair one

(Left) three-time champion Hale Irwin watches the flight of Colin Montgomerie's drive . Curtis Strange (above) came within a single stroke of joining Els, Montgomerie and Loren Roberts in the play-off

to those who have won the US Open in glorious fashion – Tom Watson's win at Pebble Beach immediately springs to mind – but there was plenty of supporting evidence at Oakmont.

Tragically, it would appear that Watson can no longer 'win' any major championship for his putter always lets him down at the vital moment, as it did at Oakmont on Sunday.

Curtis Strange was the golfer who set off in Sunday's final round demonstrating the greatest

intent. He birdied the 3rd, 4th, and 5th holes to join Els in the lead. But Strange couldn't keep it going and after four successive scores of 70 he ended the day just one stroke adrift. Neither Frank Nobilo (76) nor Hale Irwin (78) could find any inspiration and so when the crunch nine holes began it had turned into a three-way contest between Els, Montgomerie and Roberts – a new name on the trophy was thus assured.

Roberts narrowly missed his putt for a par at the 2nd sudden-death hole, allowing Els to two putt for victory

At various stages in the afternoon all three looked to be heading for victory. When Montgomerie stood on the 10th tee, having played the front nine in 32, there seemed a good chance that the US Open would have its first British champion since Tony Jacklin in 1970. Monty promptly dropped shots at the 11th, 12th and 13th. After birdieing the 11th and 13th, Roberts was the leader but he later bogeyed the 15th and, crucially, the 18th where he missed a putt of no more than four feet. Els was the firm favourite when he made a brilliant three from the rough at the 15th but then he too made a mess of his finish, three-putting the 16th and hooking wildly at the 18th. The result of all this? A three-way play off. A fifth day at Oakmont.

US Open play-offs, and there have been an extraordinary number of them, are invariably an anti-climax. Nicklaus versus Palmer, believe it or not, was an anti-climax. Els versus Roberts versus Montgomerie produced far more bogeys than birdies. When the 18 holes were complete on Monday, Els and Roberts had scored 74 apiece and Montgomerie a 78: Montgomerie

hadn't survived; two sudden-death holes later, nor had Roberts.

But if this was another anti-climax, then in years to come that fact will surely be forgotten, just as the manner of Nicklaus' first win has been.

Ernie Els has followed in the footsteps of Jones, Hogan and Nicklaus. Whether in time he proves to be 'the next dominant player', or even, as some are boldly predicting, 'the next Nicklaus', one thing is certain: it was at steamy, sweltering Oakmont that Els first proved that greatness lay within his grasp.

1994 US Open

FINAL · SCORES

E Els	69	71	66	73	279	$320,000
L Roberts	76	69	64	70	279	141,828
C Montgomerie	71	65	73	70	279	141,828

(18 hole play-off scores: Els 74; Roberts 74; Montgomerie 78.
Els beat Roberts at 2nd extra hole)

C Strange	70	70	70	70	280	75,728
J Cook	73	65	73	71	282	61,318
C Dennis	71	71	70	71	283	49,485
G Norman	71	71	69	72	283	49,485
T Watson	68	73	68	74	283	49,485
D Waldorf	74	68	73	69	284	37,179
J Maggert	71	68	75	70	284	37,179
J Sluman	72	69	72	71	284	37,179
F Nobilo	69	71	68	76	284	37,179
J McGovern	73	69	74	69	285	29,767
S Hoch	72	72	70	71	285	29,767
D Edwards	73	65	75	72	285	29,767
F Couples	72	71	69	74	286	25,899
S Lowery	71	71	68	76	286	25,899
S Verplank	70	72	75	70	287	22,477
S Ballesteros	72	72	70	73	287	22,477
H Irwin	69	69	71	78	287	22,477
S Torrance	72	71	76	69	288	19,464
S Pate	74	66	71	77	288	19,464
B Langer	72	72	73	72	289	17,223
K Triplett	70	71	71	77	289	17,223
M Springer	74	72	73	71	290	14,705
C Parry	78	68	71	73	290	14,705
C Beck	73	73	70	74	290	14,705
D Love III	74	72	74	72	292	11,514
J Furyk	74	69	74	75	292	11,514
L Clements	73	71	73	75	292	11,514
J Nicklaus	69	70	77	76	292	11,514
M Ozaki	70	73	69	80	292	11,514
M Carnevale	75	72	76	70	293	9,578
T Lehman	77	68	73	75	293	9,578
F Allen	73	70	74	76	293	9,578
T Kite	73	71	72	77	293	9,578
B Crenshaw	71	74	70	78	293	9,578

Ernie Els becomes the youngest winner of the US Open since Jerry Pate in 1976

B Faxon	73	69	71	80	293	9,578
B Hughes	71	72	77	74	294	8,005
P Baker	73	73	73	75	294	8,005
G Brand Jnr	73	71	73	77	294	8,005
B Jobe	72	74	68	80	294	8,005
F Quinn Jnr	75	72	73	75	295	7,222
P Goydos	74	72	79	71	296	6,595
F Funk	74	71	74	77	296	6,595
D Walsworth	71	75	73	77	296	6,595
T Dunlavey	76	70	78	73	297	5,105
O Browne	74	73	77	73	297	5,105
B Lane	77	70	76	74	297	5,105
M Emery	74	73	75	75	297	5,105
D Berganio	73	72	76	76	297	5,105
J Gallagher Jnr	74	68	77	78	297	5,105
W Levi	76	70	73	78	297	5,105
P Mickelson	75	70	73	79	297	5,105
T Armour III	73	73	79	73	298	4,324
H Royer III	72	71	77	78	298	4,324
S Simpson	74	73	73	78	298	4,324
S Richardson	74	73	76	76	299	4,105
F Zoeller	76	70	76	77	299	4,105
D Rummells	71	74	82	74	301	3,967
D Martin	76	70	74	81	301	3,967
E Humenik	74	72	81	75	302	3,800
M Smith	74	73	78	77	302	3,800

ERNIE ELS: THE NEXT DOMINANT PLAYER?

A Commentary by Tim Rosaforte

He was sitting in the Dormie House at Gleneagles, surrounded by an entourage of family and friends who travelled all the way from South Africa to Scotland just to see him play golf. A pint of lager was in one hand and he wore a child's frown on his boyish face. This was the US Open champion three weeks after his play-off victory at Oakmont, and Ernie Els was not a happy young man.

He just missed the cut in the Scottish Open, hooking his drive over a sandhill and into the gorse on the 18th hole at the King's course. US Open champions are not supposed to miss cuts. 'He's very hard on himself,' explained his father, Neels.

The night before, Els bemoaned his new fate as golf's new hero. What came out of that conversation with Graham Spiers from Scotland on Sunday was a revelation: at 24, Theodore Ernest Els could no longer be the lad from Johannesburg who walked a street or opened the door to a pub unnoticed. As an Open champion, the innocence of those days was gone forever. His life was no longer his. He surrendered it at Oakmont. 'I don't want to be a bloody superstar,' Els told Spiers. 'I hate all this attention. I hate the sudden fuss of it all. It's not me, I just want to be with my friends. I want to be able to hang out with the boys. I want to be able to be the person I always have been. Truly, I detest this superstar business.'

Fame may not be why Ernie Els plays golf, but fame is what Ernie Els achieved in 1994. In January he won the Desert Classic in Dubai by six strokes over Greg Norman for his first victory on the European Tour. In June he survived his own erratic driving and an 18-hole play-off against Colin Montgomerie and Loren Roberts in the US Open. In October he won the World Matchplay Championship at Wentworth and in November he shot 65 in the final round, came from four strokes back, and ran away with the inaugural Sarazen World Open Championship for a payoff of $350,000. At 24, he went from rising star to risen star.

Curtis Strange called Els the 'next God' of golf. Gary Player compared his swing to Sam Snead's. Nick Price said the last prodigy with this kind of talent was Seve Ballesteros. Arnold Palmer liked the kid's 'I'll show you' qualities. Bernhard Langer said, 'Ernie is one of the brightest talents we have in world golf. He has a great build, he hits the ball a tremendous distance, he has good rhythm and he does not get upset. Basically he has it all.'

Now comes the hard part. Living up to the predictions and accolades. Els is only the fifth player since World War II to win a major championship before turning 25. Ballesteros, who was 22 when he won the 1979 British Open, won four more majors before hitting the wall at age 32. Player was 23 when he won the '59 British, his first of nine majors. Jack Nicklaus won three of his 18 majors before he turned 25. In the pre-Els foursome, only Jerry Pate, who won the US Open at 22, has not won another major.

Els appears to have all the physical and mental attributes needed to become golf's next dominant player. And he seems savvy enough to handle the acclaim and balance the demands. By year's end, he was comfortable in his role among the superstars of golf's theatre. 'He's got his head screwed on right,' says Price, 'He'll figure it out.'

Figuring out the game of golf came easy for Els. He started learning the game at age four by pulling his father's trolley around Kempton Park in Johannesburg. His flowing rhythm came from gripping down the shafts of Neels Els' clubs. At 13, Els had already earned his Springbok colours. When he won the South African Mini Masters in 1983, Price returned after winning the World Series of Golf to present the winning trophy. Els still has the autograph on a visor at his parents' home. 'Eleven years later he wins the US Open and I win the British Open', Price said after his triumph at Turnberry. 'Isn't that amazing?'

What's amazing is how quickly Els progressed once he decided to give up tennis, rugby, cricket and football to concentrate totally on golf. At 14, he won his age division in the Optimist Junior World championship in California. At 16, he became the youngest player to win the South African Amateur. At 19, he won the South African tour school title.

It wasn't until 1991 that Els experienced hard times on the golf course. Playing the Ben Hogan Tour in the United States, Els grew terribly homesick and earned only $6,143 in eight events. He returned home a beaten man, but that difficult period was a big part of Els' maturation. Missing cuts and staying at roadside motels gave him a sobering dose of reality. 'Those guys are survivors out there', Els said. 'They play for a living, and they kicked my butt.'

The search for consistency brought Ernie Els to David Leadbetter. The famous teaching pro didn't get too technical with Els. To minimise the vicious hooks, Leadbetter had Els rotate his grip and adjust his weight shift. There wasn't much more to it. In 1992, Els burst into the international limelight by winning six events on the Sunshine Tour including the South African Masters, Open and PGA titles. The last person to win that country's triple crown was

Player, 13 years earlier.

In the fall of 1993, Els shot four rounds in the 60s to win the Dunlop Phoenix tournament in Japan. Two months later, Norman threw four rounds in the 60s at him in Dubai but could never make up the ground Els created with an opening 61. Playing together in the final round, Norman observed, 'He's got a lot calmer temperament than I had 14 years ago. I wasn't on an even-keel then. It's taken me 14 years to get to where he is now.'

At six foot three, 210 pounds, Els always seems to have 30 yards in reserve. At Oakmont, his strength was able to carry shots onto greens from thick Open roughs. At the 72nd hole, after rescuing himself from a hooked tee shot, Els made the same putt Roberts had earlier missed to join the play-off. On Monday, Els started bogey 5 – triple bogey 7, but rallied and made a gut-twisting putt on the 90th hole to send the play-off into sudden death. He won with a par on the 92nd hole. 'In the play-off, you could just see that the guy is mature beyond his years,' Price said.

Player has seen it all along. At Turnberry, after they played their first practice rounds together, the prediction was made that Els would win many major championships. There are horses for courses, and Player touted Els at Augusta, and at St Andrews, where the 1995 Open will be played. An astounding Nicklausean statistic to back up Player's prediction: in 10 majors, Els has finished in the top-10 five times.

'He showed me what I used to see in Jack Nicklaus,' Player said. 'Jack could play badly and still get the ball in the hole and win. That to me is more impressive than long drives and all the other things that matter. He holed that putt on the last hole at Oakmont. The great ones don't miss 'em, and Ernie is going to be a great one.'

Some would say he already is.

THE OPEN
CHAMPIONSHIP

THE OPEN CHAMPIONSHIP

ROLL · OF · HONOUR

1860	Willie Park	1902	Alexander Herd
1861	Tom Morris, Sr	1903	Harry Vardon
1862	Tom Morris, Sr	1904	Jack White
1863	Willie Park	1905	James Braid
1864	Tom Morris, Sr	1906	James Braid
1865	Andrew Strath	1907	Arnaud Massy
1866	Willie Park	1908	James Braid
1867	Tom Morris, Sr	1909	John H. Taylor
1868	Tom Morris, Jr	1910	James Braid
1869	Tom Morris, Jr		
1870	Tom Morris, Jr		
1871	No championships played		
1872	Tom Morris, Jr		
1873	Tom Kidd		
1874	Mungo Park		
1875	Willie Park		
1876	Bob Martin		
1877	Jamie Anderson		
1878	Jamie Anderson		
1879	Jamie Anderson		
1880	Robert Ferguson		
1881	Robert Ferguson		
1882	Robert Ferguson		
1883	* Willie Fernie		
1884	Jack Simpson		
1885	Bob Martin		
1886	David Brown		
1887	Willie Park, Jr		
1888	Jack Burns		
1889	* Willie Park, Jr		
1890	John Ball		
1891	Hugh Kirkaldy		
1892	Harold H. Hilton		
1893	William Auchterlonie		
1894	John H. Taylor		
1895	John H. Taylor		
1896	* Harry Vardon		
1897	Harold H. Hilton		
1898	Harry Vardon		
1899	Harry Vardon		
1900	John H. Taylor		
1901	James Braid		

1911	Harry Vardon
1912	Edward Ray
1913	John H. Taylor
1914	Harry Vardon
1915-19	No championships played
1920	George Duncan
1921	* Jock Hutchison
1922	Walter Hagen
1923	Arthur G. Havers

1924	Walter Hagen	1937	Henry Cotton	1987	Nick Faldo
1925	James M. Barnes	1938	R. A. Whitcombe	1988	Seve Ballesteros
1926	Robert T. Jones	1939	Richard Burton	1989	* Mark Calcavecchia
1927	Robert T. Jones	1940-45	No championships played	1990	Nick Faldo
1928	Walter Hagen	1946	Sam Snead	1991	Ian Baker-Finch
1929	Walter Hagen	1947	Fred Daly	1992	Nick Faldo
1930	Robert T. Jones	1948	Henry Cotton	1993	Greg Norman
1931	Tommy D. Armour	1949	* Bobby Locke	1994	Nick Price
1932	Gene Sarazen	1950	Bobby Locke		

1933 * Denny Shute
1934 Henry Cotton
1935 Alfred Perry
1936 Alfred Padgham

1951 Max Faulkner
1952 Bobby Locke
1953 Ben Hogan
1954 Peter Thomson
1955 Peter Thomson
1956 Peter Thomson
1957 Bobby Locke
1958 * Peter Thomson
1959 Gary Player
1960 Kel Nagle
1961 Arnold Palmer
1962 Arnold Palmer
1963 * Bob Charles
1964 Tony Lema
1965 Peter Thomson
1966 Jack Nicklaus
1967 Roberto De Vicenzo
1968 Gary Player
1969 Tony Jacklin
1970 * Jack Nicklaus
1971 Lee Trevino
1972 Lee Trevino
1973 Tom Weiskopf
1974 Gary Player
1975 * Tom Watson
1976 Johnny Miller
1977 Tom Watson
1978 Jack Nicklaus
1979 Seve Ballesteros
1980 Tom Watson
1981 Bill Rogers
1982 Tom Watson
1983 Tom Watson
1984 Seve Ballesteros
1985 Sandy Lyle
1986 Greg Norman

* Winner in play-off.

· HIGHLIGHTS ·

MOST WINS:

6 Harry Vardon
5 Hohn H. Taylor
James Braid
Peter Thomson
Tom Watson

MOST TIMES RUNNER-UP:

7 Jack Nicklaus

BIGGEST MARGIN OF VICTORY:

13 Old Tom Morris (1862)

LOWEST WINNING TOTAL:

267 Greg Norman (1993)

LOWEST SINGLE ROUND:

63 Mark Hayes (1977)
Isao Aoki (1980)
Greg Norman (1986)
Paul Broadhurst (1990)
Jodie Mudd (1991)
Nick Faldo (1993)
Payne Stewart (1993)

LOWEST FINAL ROUND BY WINNER:

64 Greg Norman (1993)
65 Tom Watson (1977)
Severiano Ballesteros (1988)

OLDEST CHAMPION:

Old Tom Morris,
aged 46 (1867)

YOUNGEST CHAMPION:

Young Tom Morris,
aged 17 (1868)
Severiano Ballesteros
(youngest this century,
aged 22 in 1979)

THE 1994 OPEN CHAMPIONSHIP

After the oppressive heat and humidity of Oakmont almost anywhere would have felt refreshing but the atmosphere at Turnberry was positively inspiring

Few championships had been as eagerly awaited as the 1994 Open. The 'British Open', as Americans like to call it, was coming to Scotland's Ayrshire Coast – Burns Country – and more than that, it was being held at Turnberry, that jewel of a golf course where Nicklaus and Watson fought out their 'Duel in the Sun'. The 1977 championship, Turnberry's first, was perhaps the greatest of all Opens and in 1986, Turnberry's second and only other staging, Greg Norman produced arguably the greatest ever round in an Open, his second day 63 having been compiled in quite testing conditions.

In July 1994 Turnberry had never looked better; Norman was back as the defender of the famous Claret Jug and as for Watson, well, fresh from a transatlantic stop-over at his beloved Ballybunion he was said to be striking the ball as confidently and as crisply as the Watson of 1977. Yes, eagerly awaited, all right.

The Ailsa Course was groomed to perfection for the 123rd Open Championship and the gaze of Ailsa Craig was as mesmeric as ever. When the skies are blue and the sun is shining Turnberry's setting appears so wondrous that it invites comparison with the great courses of the Monterey Peninsula (although as any Scotsman will remind you, there are no burns

Greg Norman returns to the scene of his first major

and no pot bunkers at Pebble Beach). The skies were blue and the sun was shining on the first morning of the 1994 Open Championship.

Not surprisingly, the early starters made the most of the benign conditions and, as happens every year at the start of the Open, a few unfamiliar names appeared at the top of the leaderboard. European Tour rookie, Jonathan Lomas, playing in his first Open, returned a four under par 66 and American Andrew Magee, a 67. Watson, who in contrast to Lomas was playing in his 20th consecutive championship, teed off very early and began with an encouraging 68. Around midday, however, the weather began to change: the blue skies turned to grey and a friendly zephyr was transformed into an unfriendly wind; Watson's 68 suddenly looked a very good score. John Daly managed to match it, though, much to the delight of his vast, adoring gallery but then 'Long John's performance was eclipsed by Greg 'Two Eagles' Turner. It was a shortish putt that gained the New Zealander his eagle at the par five 7th and a longish iron that achieved it at the par four 16th – a two iron, in fact, hit straight into the wind and straight into the hole from 178 yards. Turner finished with a 65 which nobody could equal. At the end of the first round he found himself four ahead of Nick Price and Ernie Els; five ahead of Ballesteros, six ahead of Norman and 10 ahead of Nick Faldo. A 75 for Faldo? The three-time champion experienced a wretched day, the most wretched moment of which was when he played the wrong ball from out of the rough at the 17th, so incurring a two stroke penalty (and a few swishes later he was writing down an eight for that hole). It was not, as the Englishman put it, 'The cleverest thing I've ever done in my life'.

The friendly zephyr returned on Friday morning but this time refused to be chased away. Low scoring was very much the order of the day, indeed, those who failed to break 70 in the second round lost significant ground.

Friday was a glorious day for Tom Watson. It was vintage Watson too, for he didn't just strike the ball as crisply and as confidently as the Huckleberry Finn lookalike we remembered from '77, he actually scored like

Watson dons his links attire and resumes his quest for a record-equalling sixth Open title

him. Six birdies in his first eleven holes guided Watson to a 65. 'Not bad for a 44 year old has been', he concluded.

With Turner taking 71 and Lomas 70, Watson's seven under par, two round total of 133 gave him a one stroke lead in the championship. Sweden's Jesper Parnevik and the American Brad Faxon were his closest pursuers, then came Nick Price, just two behind after an impressive 66. Greg Norman

next brought him crashing to earth. 'Killer Whale in beach drama', ran one headline the following day. Among other interesting, if less turbulent rounds on Friday was the 66 of Fuzzy Zoeller, which included four twos, and the 66 of Nick Faldo which comprised four birdies and 14 pars. Faldo not only demonstrated his immense courage but also his enormous pride, for had he failed to break 70 (following the disastrous 75 on Thursday) it would have

The calm before the storm. John Daly shared the lead early on the second day; Come Sunday, however, he was propping up the entire field scored a 67 to be on 138, the same as Ernie Els. What news of John Daly? He should have been right up with the front runners after reaching the turn in 32 – at which point he actually shared the lead – but a hooked tee shot onto the beach at the 10th followed by four putts (one a back-handed swat) at the

meant him missing his first 36 hole cut in 18 Open Championships.

If Friday belonged to Watson, then the star performer on Saturday was Zoeller – whistling Fuzzy Zoeller – surely the most laidback golfer in the world. Forty-two year old Zoeller was enjoying a bumper season on the US Tour, his best for many a year and when it comes to major championships, Fuzzy has been there before, winning the 1979 Masters (after a play-off with Watson) and the 1984 US Open (after a play-off with Norman). Zoeller shot a sizzling 64 in the third round at Turnberry and began whistling every time he holed a birdie putt.

It is just as well that the rest of the field didn't copy his habit for the result would have been deafening: once again Turnberry's defences were being continually breached. So

where was the buffeting wind? Where was the unpredictable bounce? This was a Scottish links for goodness sake! The old tale that claimed, 'If you can see Ailsa Craig it's going to rain and if you cannot see it, it's raining already' was exposed as a lie. With seemingly everyone making birdies in the third round the 69s of Norman and Els and the 70 of Faldo just

(Above left) Nick Faldo went from the ridiculous to the sublime, scoring a calamitous 75 on Thursday and a sparkling 64 on Sunday (Above right) Greg Turner was the championship leader after 18 holes

weren't good enough to put them into a challenging position. Above them, and now effectively out of range, were the leaders after 54 holes – six players separated by a single stroke: Zoeller (64) and Faxon (67) led on 201, with Price (67), Watson (69), Parnevik (68) and Rafferty (65) on 202. As several others were only a handful of strokes behind it had developed into the most genuinely 'open' championship for years. Still, there had to be

compiled, so it seemed, with minimal fuss (one hesitates to use the word effortlessly) and Price looked ready to pounce. Twice he had come close to winning the Open, first in 1982 and again in 1988; he was a much more accomplished player now – perhaps the best in the world – but could he time his run to perfection?

For 10 years Tom Watson has been dreaming of a 6th Open victory. The image of

After scoring 69-66-67 Nick Price was perfectly placed going into Sunday's final round

an overnight favourite, and if the heart said Watson, then the head said Price.

Rather like the canny middle distance runner who tucks himself in behind the race leader, patiently waiting to pounce, Nick Price appeared to be ideally placed on Saturday evening. Rounds of 69-66-67 had been

his illjudged approach to the 17th at St Andrews in 1984 is almost as clear as the image of Ballesteros holing his winning putt on the 18th green. He knows that he has never been the same golfer since and at Turnberry he knew that it was one thing to be striking the ball like the Watson of 1977 and another to be putting like the Watson of 1977. Sadly on the final day of the 1994 championship the golfing world witnessed more than a little of the former but barely a trace of the latter. Watson took 38 putts on Sunday.

The logjam at the top of the leaderboard remained intact for nine holes but was shattered when Jesper Parnevik unleashed a hatrick of birdies from the 11th. With Rafferty and Faxon both struggling, and Zoeller unable to raise much of a whistle, it became apparent that only Price could prevent an historic Swedish victory. Parnevik bogeyed the 15th but when more birdies came at the 16th and 17th

The American challenge failed to materialise on the final day: both Faxon (above right) and Watson (below right) struggled, while Fuzzy Zoeller could do no better than a level par 70. Instead, it was left to Sweden's Jesper Parnevik (left) and Zimbabwean Nick Price to battle it out for the coveted Claret Jug

Price eagles the 71st hole and nearly 'jumps out of his skin'. It's over! The champion hugs his caddie, Jeff 'Squeaky' Medlen at the end of an improbable afternoon

he looked unstoppable.

Jesper Parnevik, Open champion? Not yet. Price's response and, yes, his timing, was truly amazing. Even now, when the dust has long since settled, it seems hard to believe that he pulled it off. If ever anyone snatched victory from the jaws of defeat it was Nick Price in the 1994 Open. It is true that he was assisted by the failure of Parnevik's bold strategy at the 18th, which resulted in a dropped shot rather than the birdie he had intended (and mistakenly believed necessary) but to play the last three holes of a major championship in three under par – *when he knew that he had to* – was extraordinary. It was, of course, the mark of a champion. Price birdied the 16th, eagled the 17th with a putt of fully 50 feet and then parred the final hole for a one stroke victory. 'In 1982 I had my left hand on the trophy; in 1988 I had my right hand on it; now I have got both hands on it – and does it feel good!'

1994 OPEN CHAMPIONSHIP

FINAL · SCORES

**Nick Price,
1994 Open
Champion**

Player	R1	R2	R3	R4	Total	Prize
N Price	69	66	67	66	268	£110,000
J Parnevik	68	66	68	67	269	88,000
F Zoeller	71	66	64	70	271	74,000
A Forsbrand	72	71	66	64	273	50,666
M James	72	67	66	68	273	50,666
D Feherty	68	69	66	70	273	50,666
B Faxon	69	65	67	73	274	36,000
N Faldo	75	66	70	64	275	30,000
T Kite	71	69	66	69	275	30,000
C Montgomerie	72	69	65	69	275	30,000
R Claydon	72	71	68	65	276	19,333
M McNulty	71	70	68	67	276	19,333
F Nobilo	69	67	72	68	276	19,333
J Lomas	66	70	72	68	276	19,333
M Calcavecchia	71	70	67	68	276	19,333
G Norman	71	67	69	69	276	19,333
L Mize	73	69	64	70	276	19,333
T Watson	68	65	69	74	276	19,333
R Rafferty	71	66	65	74	276	19,333
M Brooks	74	64	71	68	277	12,500
V Singh	70	68	69	70	277	12,500
G Turner	65	71	70	71	277	12,500
P Senior	68	71	67	71	277	12,500
B Estes	72	68	72	66	278	7,972
T Price	74	65	71	68	278	7,972
P Lawrie	71	69	70	68	278	7,972
J Maggert	69	74	67	68	278	7,972
T Lehman	70	69	70	69	278	7,972
E Els	69	69	69	71	278	7,972
M Springer	72	67	68	71	278	7,972
L Roberts	68	69	69	72	278	7,972
P Jacobsen	69	70	67	72	278	7,972
C Stadler	71	69	66	72	278	7,972
A Coltart	71	69	66	72	278	7,972
M Davis	75	68	69	67	279	6,700
L Janzen	74	69	69	67	279	6,700
G Evans	69	69	73	68	279	6,700
J M Olazabal	72	71	69	68	280	6,100
D Hospital	72	69	71	68	280	6,100
D Gilford	72	68	72	68	280	6,100
S Ballesteros	70	70	71	69	280	6,100
B Marchbank	71	70	70	69	280	6,100
D Clarke	73	68	69	70	280	6,100
J Van de Velde	68	70	71	71	280	6,100
D Love III	71	67	68	74	280	6,100
M Ozaki	69	71	66	74	280	6,100
J Gallagher Jnr	73	68	69	71	281	5,450
D Edwards	68	68	73	72	281	5,450
G Kraft	69	74	66	72	281	5,450
H Twitty	71	72	66	72	281	5,450
D Frost	70	71	71	70	282	4,925
M Lanner	69	74	69	70	282	4,925
K Tomori	69	69	73	71	282	4,925
T Watanabe	72	71	68	71	282	4,925
P Baker	71	72	70	70	283	4,700
J Cook	73	67	70	73	283	4,700
T Nakajima	73	68	69	73	283	4,700
B Watts	68	70	71	74	283	4,700
R McFarlane	68	74	67	74	283	4,700
L Clements	72	71	72	70	285	4,050
C Mason	69	71	73	72	285	4,050
R Alvarez	70	72	71	72	285	4,050
W Bennett	72	67	74	73	286	Am.
W Riley	77	77	70	73	286	3,900
S Lyle	71	72	72	72	287	3,900

TOM WATSON: IF ONLY HE COULD PUTT...

A Commentary by John Hopkins

Nick Price won the Open in style. There is no denying that. If a true champion is someone who is able to summon up some extra wizardry when it is needed, then Price did just that at Turnberry. Am I alone, however, in wishing that the 123rd Open could have gone to a freckle-faced American with a gap-toothed grin? By that I mean Tom Watson.

Let me confess my allegiances. Watson is a man I greatly admire – as I know do many others. The Scots think that he could only be improved if he had been born in Kirkcaldy and supported Raith Rovers.

Watson is, in some ways, more British than the British. During an Open at Royal Birkdale he was spotted queuing for fish and chips one night. He dresses for dinner, has little difficulty in driving on the left and does not complain about warm beer and a lack of air conditioning. 'Tom loves Britain,' Linda Watson, his wife, said. 'He thinks the people are so courteous and polite to us in a way that, unfortunately, they are not at home.' Watson later confirmed this. 'Britain is the last civilised country,' he told me.

He is a traditionalist, one who understands that a purpose of golf is to test your honesty and integrity as much as your skill and courage. Play hard but abide by the rules is Watson's creed. So the sight of this man who understands so well the complicated British sporting psyche, who comes to these shores with pleasure and without any hint of complaint at any inefficiency he might find, in contention for the Open was too much to bear. The Scots wanted him to win. I wanted him to win. In their heart of hearts, I think some of the players wanted him to win, too.

And he had won – at Turnberry in 1977 in one of the most famous Opens of all time, the second of his five Open victories. So he knew the course, had experienced the pressure. Everything was right for him to equal Harry Vardon's six victories. Except for his putting.

Watson's putting is to him what his heel was to Achilles and cigars and brandy were to Winston Churchill. To say it is a weakness is to be guilty of understatement. It is almost unbearable to see how well Watson strikes the ball from tee to green and how miserably he putts when the pressure is on. 'I have never seen Tom hit the ball better,' Bruce Edwards, his caddie, said during the Open. 'There is a calmness about him now.' But you could have wept at the way the ball would not go into the hole on the last afternoon of the Open.

There he was, leading a legion of spectators around as he began the final round one stroke behind Brad Faxon and Fuzzy Zoeller, the overnight leaders. By the 9th, the 63rd hole, Watson was done for, the murder weapon being his putter which resolutely refused to obey what his eyes and head and those of all Watson's supporters, too, told it. He took three putts on the 8th and again on the 9th and that was it. Another Open had passed him by. How many more chances would he get? He was 44. Time was running out.

That night a revealing little cameo took place on the par three course in the grounds of the Turnberry Hotel. Present were Watson, with a cigar in his mouth, Linda, and Jack and Barbara Nicklaus. They had eaten dinner together, shared some good wine and now it was time for mixed foursomes.

Nicklaus urged Linda Watson to chip accurately. 'Whatever you do don't leave the ball four feet away,' he said. Watson laughed then but he could have cried a few hours earlier. Four feet is not his range. It is a distance he and his putter cannot comprehend, like a child confronted by a piece of algebra. He can hit a two iron 220 yards through the air so that it feathers down softly on the green and ends ten feet from the flag. But expect him to hole a putt from 48 inches and you might as well ask how many angels can dance on the head of a pin.

To make it worse, the 1994 Watson is arguably a more complete player in every department except putting than the Watson of old. He is calmer, as Edwards attests. That cool analytical streak has improved. He is a better ball striker. He knows his limitations. He has nothing left to prove except how good he is.

And he did that with a vengeance in 1994 finishing better in the four major championships than any other player, José-Maria Olazabal and Ernie Els included. Watson came 13th at Augusta, sixth in the US Open at Oakmont, joint 11th at Turnberry and ninth at Southern Hills in the USPGA. His average finishing position was ninth compared with the 16th of Ernie Els, the next best player. Nick Price and Olazabal failed to make the cut at the US Open.

For Watson, the pattern always seemed to be the same. He would play beautifully for 54 holes and find himself in a position just behind the leaders, close enough to frighten them. Then his putting troubles – his flinches he calls them – would get the better of him and he would fall away. At the US Masters, the US Open and the Open he concluded with rounds of 74.

At the end at Turnberry Watson looked close to tears. His hands twirled relentlessly, a manifestation of his inner turmoil. 'It really hurts,' he admitted quietly. 'It hurts inside.' It hurt Linda Watson just as much from her favourite vantage position just behind the ropes. 'It's kind of hard for me to understand why he is so afraid of putting,' she said after the Open. 'When he's relaxed he is one of the best. He will break through again but every year it gets harder.'

Watson is proud. You can see that by the angle of his head, the jaunty walk, the way he conducts himself. In those moments at Turnberry when he must have felt truly wretched and despairing, there was little outward sign of it. He maintained his composure, demonstrated a dignified bearing even though the anguish he was suffering must have been made worse by his memories of the famous Scottish course.

In 1977 he had run in a huge putt near the climax of that tumultuous last round. Now he had to listen to the roars that greeted Price's holing an equally long putt on the 17th.

It is so hard to improve when middle age wraps its tentacles around you. Yet Watson has done just that. He has defied convention and for a time at Turnberry it looked as though he might turn the clock back. If only he could putt!

Nicklaus did it at Augusta at the age of 46. When it was thought he was a spent force, he won the Masters. Ray Floyd won a US Open when he was Watson's age, as did Hale Irwin. There would not have been a more popular winner at Turnberry this summer than Thomas Sturges Watson. He has the heart of a lion, the mind of a champion.

For years the putter was the club that saved him and was instrumental in his winning so many victories. Now it is the club that is the undoing of him. What was once a wand in his hands is now a sledgehammer. It is stopping him claiming what is rightfully his.

There is no justice in this world.

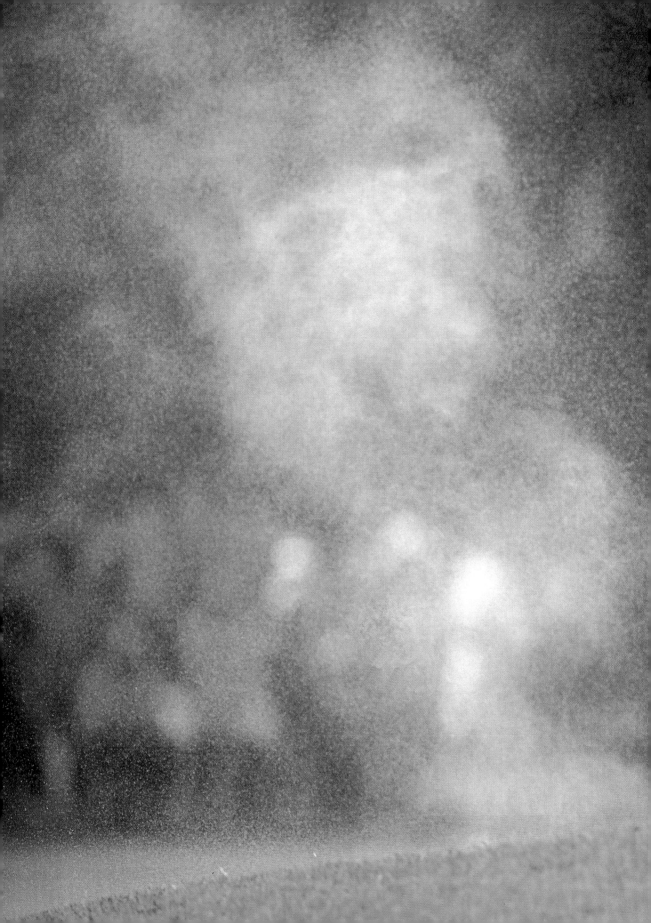

THE USPGA

THE USPGA

ROLL · OF · HONOUR

1916	James M. Barnes	1952	Jim Turnesa	1987	* Larry Nelson
1917-18	No championships played	1953	Walter Burkemo	1988	Jeff Sluman
1919	James M. Barnes	1954	Chick Harbert	1989	Payne Stewart
1920	Jock Hutchison	1955	Doug Ford	1990	Wayne Grady
1921	Walter Hagen	1956	Jack Burke	1991	John Daly
1922	Gene Sarazen	1957	Lionel Hebert	1992	Nick Price
1923	Gene Sarazen	1958	Dow Finsterwald	1993	* Paul Azinger
1924	Walter Hagen	1959	Bob Rosburg	1994	Nick Price
1925	Walter Hagen	1960	Jay Hebert		* Winner in play-off.
1926	Walter Hagen	1961	* Jerry Barber		
1927	Walter Hagen	1962	Gary Player		
1928	Leo Diegel	1963	Jack Nicklaus		
1929	Leo Diegel	1964	Bobby Nichols		
1930	Tommy Armour	1965	Dave Marr		
1931	Tom Creavy	1966	Al Geiberger		
1932	Olin Dutra	1967	* Don January		
1933	Gene Sarazen	1968	Julius Boros		
1934	Paul Runyan	1969	Ray Floyd		
1935	Johnny Revolta	1970	Dave Stockton		
1936	Denny Shute	1971	Jack Nicklaus		
1937	Denny Shute	1972	Gary Player		
1938	Paul Runyan	1973	Jack Nicklaus		
1939	Henry Picard	1974	Lee Trevino		
1940	Byron Nelson	1975	Jack Nicklaus		
1941	Vic Ghezzi	1976	Dave Stockton		
1942	Sam Snead	1977	* Lanny Wadkins		
1943	No championship played	1978	* John Mahaffey		
1944	Bob Hamilton	1979	* David Graham		
1945	Byron Nelson	1980	Jack Nicklaus		
1946	Ben Hogan	1981	Larry Nelson		
1947	Jim Ferrier	1982	Ray Floyd		
1948	Ben Hogan	1983	Hal Sutton		
1949	Sam Snead	1984	Lee Trevino		
1950	Chandler Harper	1985	Hubert Green		
1951	Sam Snead	1986	Bob Tway		

· HIGHLIGHTS ·

MOST WINS:

5 Walter Hagen

Jack Nicklaus

MOST TIMES RUNNER-UP:

4 Jack Nicklaus

BIGGEST MARGIN OF VICTORY:

7 Jack Nicklaus (1980)

6 Nick Price (1994)

LOWEST WINNING TOTAL:

269 Nick Price (1994)

LOWEST SINGLE ROUND:

63 Bruce Crampton (1975)

Ray Floyd (1982)

Gary Player (1984)

Vijay Singh (1993)

LOWEST FINAL ROUND BY WINNER:

65 David Graham (1979)

Jeff Sluman (1988)

OLDEST CHAMPION:

Julius Boros, aged 48 (1968)

YOUNGEST CHAMPION:

Gene Sarazen, aged 20 (1922)

THE 1994 USPGA

A fortnight after his thrilling victory at Turnberry, Nick Price attempted to
become the first player to win successive Majors since Tom Watson in 1982 and the first
to achieve the British Open-USPGA double since Walter Hagen in 1924

Oklahoma, 'Where the corn is as high as
an elephant's eye', and where in
August the climate is unbearable.
Welcome to Tulsa; welcome to
Southern Hills and welcome to the
76th USPGA Championship.

The name Southern Hills is misleading. The
course is built in a dust bowl and there are no
proper hills to speak of, just plenty of trees,
tight fairways and savage rough – in other
words it is a typical US Open-USPGA type
venue. Here is where Hubert Green survived a
death threat to win the 1977 US Open and
where Ray Floyd claimed his second USPGA
title in 1982. Here too is where Arnold Palmer
nearly won the USPGA back in 1970.

Twenty-four years on Palmer was back at
Southern Hills embarking on what he had
decided would be his final appearance in the
one major championship he never won. Just as
it was an emotional experience for Palmer, the
same can be said for the presence of title
holder Paul Azinger. This was Azinger's first
major tournament since his victory at Inverness
in 1993 – and since the subsequent discovery
that he had cancer in his shoulder.

And how different this 1994 USPGA was
from that 1993 championship! Then, Azinger
had triumphed after a dramatic play-off with

**Paul Azinger made an emotional return to the
USPGA Championship at Southern Hills**

Nick Price
swept clear of
the field with a
brilliant 65 on
Friday

Greg Norman and at the end of a marvellous afternoon during which the lead switched back and forth between Azinger, Norman and Nick Faldo. As majors go, it was nothing short of a classic. Southern Hills, 1994 could never be described as such; in its way, however, it was certainly memorable and arguably more significant. The story of the 76th USPGA Championship is a tale of domination.

When Nick Price arrived at Southern Hills everyone was still talking about that putt – the enormous one he made for an eagle at the 71st hole in the British Open.

Yet if the 37 year old Zimbabwean was very good at Turnberry, he was great at Southern Hills. In short, he led from start to finish and set a new championship record in the process. Price's four round total of 269 was the lowest ever score in an American major. He bogeyed the final hole but still won by six strokes. It was an awesome display and one which confirmed him as the world's number one golfer. Even the modest Price was now prepared to accept that accolade. In the space of just two years he had amassed 16 victories worldwide, including three majors, and the best part of six million dollars in prize money. Clearly, life can begin at 35.

(Left) Arnold Palmer calls it a day. (Below left) Nick Faldo repeated his Turnberry experience of starting slowly but finishing strongly. (Below right) Montgomerie scored a 67 in the first round to tie Nick Price for the lead

To set the record straight, Price merely shared the lead after the first round: Colin Montgomerie matched his opening three under par 67; Ernie Els, Fred Couples, Ian Woosnam and Phil Mickelson all returned 68s and there were eight players on 69. It was on the second day that Price spread-eagled the field.

With a brilliant round of 65, the newly crowned British Open champion established a five stroke lead after 36 holes: 67 + 65 = 132.

better than anyone since Ben Hogan', declared Ben Crenshaw, who along with Corey Pavin and Jay Haas was tied for second place on 137. The rest of the field was beginning to string out across Oklahoma: Olazabal, the winner of the Masters was on 138; Els, the US Open champion was on 139 while Faldo and Norman were on 140.

Now of course, even Nick Price is permitted the occasional day off – or rather off-day

Corey Pavin impressed at Southern Hills but still finished a distant second to Price

It was a blistering pace forged in blistering conditions. Lauren St John wrote in *The Sunday Times*, 'A sense of inevitability now attaches to the name of Nick Price... No sooner does it appear on the leaderboard than it rises inexorably to the top'. So impressive was Price's golf that many of his peers seemed almost willing to concede him the famous Wanamaker Trophy. 'He's striking the ball

(when judged by his mighty standards) and in the third round he compiled a level par round of 70. He didn't hit the ball with his usual authority but nevertheless could rely on a still razor sharp short game. In truth, Price scrambled more than a little on Saturday but he never lost control. Anyway, it was what happened the next day that mattered. And Sunday was anything but an off-day.

Phil Mickelson
gained his first
top three finish
in a major
championship

On the final afternoon of the final major of 1994, the man of the moment set off to play 'the best nine holes of my life'.

The chasing pack had finally started to chase a little on Saturday. Haas moved to within three of the lead after 54 holes; Mickelson and Pavin were four behind and Norman was five off the pace. The Great White Shark still harboured a glimmer of hope and he duly birdied the 1st and 2nd holes on Sunday.

The vast gallery wondered if he was about to launch a final round assault. He wasn't – besides (and perhaps because) Price's response was to birdie the 3rd and 4th. Haas faded badly, and as neither Pavin nor Mickelson could mount a serious challenge, Price remained firmly in control. With a third birdie at the 8th he moved seven ahead of the field and from then on he simply marched – some would say strolled – triumphantly into the history books.

A victorious Price salutes the crowd after breaking Bobby Nicholls' 30 year old USPGA championship record. Price has now won more majors than Greg Norman (left)

1994 USPGA

FINAL · SCORES

Nick Price embraces the Wanamaker Trophy
for the second time in three years

N Price	67	65	70	67	269	$310,000							
C Pavin	70	67	69	69	275	160,000							
P Mickelson	68	71	67	70	276	110,000							
N Faldo	73	67	71	66	277	76,666							
G Norman	71	69	67	70	277	76,666							
J Cook	71	67	69	70	277	76,666							
S Elkington	73	70	66	69	278	57,500							
J M Olazabal	72	66	70	70	278	57,500							
I Woosnam	68	72	73	66	279	41,000							
T Kite	72	68	69	70	279	41,000							
T Watson	69	72	67	71	279	41,000							
L Roberts	69	72	67	71	279	41,000							
B Crenshaw	70	67	70	72	279	41,000							
J Haas	71	66	68	75	280	32,000	B Mayfair	73	72	71	70	286	6,030
K Triplett	71	69	71	70	281	27,000	G Morgan	71	68	73	74	286	6,030
L Mize	72	72	67	70	281	27,000	T Lehman	73	71	68	74	286	6,030
N McNulty	72	68	70	71	281	27,000	H Irwin	75	69	68	74	286	6,030
G Day	70	69	70	72	281	27,000	N Lancaster	73	72	72	70	287	5,200
C Stadler	70	70	74	68	282	18,666	D Edwards	72	70	74	71	287	5,200
M McCumber	73	70	71	68	282	18,666	D Gilford	69	73	73	72	287	5,200
F Zoeller	69	71	72	70	282	18,666	B Andrade	71	71	78	68	288	4,112
B Glasson	71	73	68	70	282	18,666	F Allem	74	67	74	73	288	4,112
C Strange	73	71	68	70	282	18,666	B Estes	72	71	72	73	288	4,112
C Parry	70	69	70	73	282	18,666	A Magee	70	74	71	73	288	4,112
B Lane	70	73	68	72	283	13,000	F Nobilo	72	67	74	75	288	4,112
B Langer	73	71	67	72	283	13,000	G Kraft	74	69	70	75	288	4,112
D Frost	70	71	69	73	283	13,000	M Ozaki	71	69	72	76	288	4,112
E Els	68	71	69	75	283	13,000	D A Weibring	69	73	70	76	288	4,112
J Sluman	70	72	66	75	283	13,000	J D Blake	72	71	74	74	291	2,600
B Faxon	72	73	73	66	284	8,458	P Stewart	72	73	72	74	291	2,600
W Grady	75	68	71	70	284	8,458	J Inman	70	72	73	76	291	2,600
B Boyd	72	71	70	71	284	8,458	T Smith	74	69	71	77	291	2,600
L Clements	74	70	69	71	284	8,458	D Hammond	74	69	76	73	292	2,512
S Torrance	69	75	69	71	284	8,458	P Senior	74	71	70	77	292	2,512
R Zokol	77	67	67	73	284	8,458	S Lyle	75	70	76	76	297	2,462
C Beck	72	70	72	71	285	7,000	D Pride	75	69	73	80	297	2,462
B McCallister	74	64	75	72	285	7,000	B Henninger	77	65	78	78	298	2,412
C Montgomerie	67	76	70	72	285	7,000	H Meshiai	74	71	74	79	298	2,412
F Couples	68	74	75	69	286	6,030	I Baker-Finch	73	69	70	76	288	2,650

Arnold Palmer: A Legend takes his Bow

A Commentary by Alistair Tait

t's really nice of you to hit the ball over here, Arnold,' said one fan to America's King of Golf as he stood over his last approach shot in his last USPGA Championship.

'I can just about hit it anywhere you want but where I'm not supposed to,' was the King's response.

There was deep resignation in Arnold Palmer's voice, a resignation which underlined the diminishing powers of America's most famous golfing statesman. The days when Palmer could manoeuvre the ball at will were long gone, his once awesome power a thing of the distant past. That was evident when he pulled out a fairway wood for his second shot to Southern Hills' 430-yard, par-4, 18th hole. Arnold Palmer would never have played a fairway wood to this hole in his heyday, let alone a fairway wood that had little chance of reaching the putting surface. 'It just absolutely amazes me that the one thing that changes is that I hit a driver on holes I used to hit a 3-wood off of - and that means I'm not hitting it as far,' said Palmer before the tournament began.

It was Palmer's last pre-tournament press conference as a player. Even though he has a lifetime exemption to play in the game's fourth major, he had finally come to the conclusion that it was time to stop chasing the elusive title standing between him and a career grand slam in the majors.

Palmer had made a similar decision prior to the US Open at Oakmont, where he had made an emotional exit from the championship that meant the most to him, and which he only

won once (at Cherry Hills in 1960). There wasn't a dry eye in the press room at Oakmont, but Arnold was more subdued this time, more reflective. He talked about missing out on the grand slam, a feat that would have enabled him to join an elite club of four players - Gene Sarazen, Ben Hogan, Gary Player and Jack Nicklaus - who have won the game's four major championships. He talked about wanting to win this one especially for his father, who had been a PGA Pro for most of his life and who taught Arnold the game. And he sought reasons for not winning. 'It's a Championship that I tried to find excuses or ways to explain why I haven't won it,' said Palmer. 'I haven't found one yet. I keep looking for them.'

Ever the statesman, Palmer did finally come up with a reason when he graciously recognised that on each occasion he had simply been bettered by a peer. 'The only excuse I can find is that a couple of times a couple of guys played a little better than I did at the right time and aced me,' said Palmer. In fact, he came close to winning the USPGA three times, finishing second in 1964, 1968 and 1970.

All in all, Arnold had played 121 rounds and recorded 8,892 strokes in pursuit of the USPGA Championship. He had made the cut 24 times in 37 attempts, but hadn't been a threat for 17 years, finishing tied for 19th spot in 1977. The great man had missed the cut in the last four championships and made only four cuts of the previous 12. The best he could do was 63rd place in 1989. It was definitely time to quit. Arnold knew it, knew he had gone on too long, knew he should have abandoned the hunt years earlier. 'My intentions are not to play in any more PGAs. Not because I don't want to, but because my game is not threatening. If it were still threatening, I would be looking to come back.'

Arnold Palmer hasn't really been a threat in any tournament for years. That's not surprising - a 64 year old man, even one as great as Arnold Palmer, can't be expected to beat players 30 years his junior. His last win on the regular US Tour came in the 1973 Bob Hope Desert Classic. His last Senior win was in 1988, in the Crestar Classic. Despite that, though, Palmer is still a major draw. And not just in America, where he is revered throughout the land, but all over the world. In an age when players like Greg Norman, Nick Faldo and Seve Ballesteros can command big endorsement fees, so can Palmer, some 20 years after his prime. Nowadays his role is that of elder statesman. That's as it should be, for if anyone has a right to comment on matters relating to the game of golf, it is Arnold Palmer. For example, given that the first three majors of 1994 were won by non-Americans, the American press were showing a xenophobic interest in who won the USPGA Championship. It was left to Palmer to remind his countrymen that golf is only bettered when players from different countries win the game's major championships. 'I don't think that the Australians or British or Africans or Japanese or whoever is winning is going to do anything but enhance the game of golf,' said Arnold when asked if he was concerned about non-Americans winning all four of the game's grand slam events.

Arnold Palmer has always sought to enhance the game of golf. He did that by his very presence in America. Thousands, if not millions, of Americans became hooked on golf simply because of him. His swashbuckling manner, his famous last round charges, his all out attacking style gripped the American imagination. Even today Arnie's Army still turn

out in their thousands when their leader tees it up. Not only did Arnold Palmer make the American game what it is today, but in some ways the British game also, for almost single handedly, he made the Open Championship the most coveted prize in golf.

Arnold's decision to play in the 1960 Centenary Open at St Andrews saved the Open from terminal decline. For years the top Americans had been passing over the chance to play in the Open. It was simply a non-event for them. Palmer changed their minds. He recognised that the Open was the true international major, saw it had a history and tradition all of its own. He didn't win the 1960 Open but he won the following year at Birkdale and came back every year after that, opening the floodgates so that today almost every top American plays in the Open Championship.

There was a great ovation as Palmer walked his final fairway in the USPGA Championship. His army had turned out in force. There were a few chants of 'Arnie, Arnie,' and even a few cries of 'You're the man.' As hackneyed and cliched as that expression is, if ever it applied to one golfer then it is to Arnold Palmer. He is 'The Man' of American Golf. Indeed, he was given the USPGA's Distinguished Service Award earlier in the week in recognition of his contribution to the American game.

Palmer never really had a chance of even making the cut in his last USPGA Championship; scores of 79-73 took care of that. But for all that the great man was still able to put on a show on the last hole. Palmer hit his fairway wood short of the 18th green and then chipped poorly to 25 feet. It seemed his last hole in the major he had never won would be a bogey. But Palmer, as he had done so often in his prime, holed the putt. The fans were delirious. They stood in unison in the hot Oklahoma sun and hailed their King. Arnold Palmer had given them their last hurrah.

3

HEINEKEN WORLD CUP

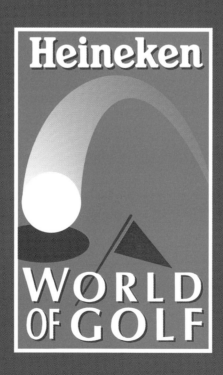

HEINEKEN WORLD CUP

ROLL · OF · HONOUR

1953	Argentina	Roberto de Vicenzo	Antonio Cerda	Beaconsfield GC, Montreal, Canada
1954	Australia	Peter Thomson	Kel Nagle	Laval-sur-le-Lac GC, Montreal, Canada
1955	United States	Ed Furgol	Chick Harbert	Columbia GC, Washington DC, USA
1956	United States	Ben Hogan	Sam Snead	Wentworth Club, Surrey, England
1957	Japan	T Nakamura	Koichi Ono	Kasumigaseki CC, Tokyo, Japan
1958	Ireland	Harry Bradshaw	Christy O'Connor	Club de Golf Mexico, Mexico
1959	Australia	Peter Thomson	Kel Nagle	Royal Melbourne GC, Melbourne, Australia
1960	United States	Arnold Palmer	Sam Snead	Portmarnock GC, Dublin, Ireland
1961	United States	Sam Snead	Jimmy Demaret	Dorado Beach GC, Dorado Beach, Puerto Rico
1962	United States	Arnold Palmer	Sam Snead	Jockey Club Golf, Buenos Aires, Argentina
1963	United States	Jack Nicklaus	Arnold Palmer	Golf de St-Nom-la-Breteche, Paris, France
1964	United States	Jack Nicklaus	Arnold Palmer	Royal Kaanapali GC, Maui, Hawaii
1965	South Africa	Gary Player	Harold Henning	RACE del Club de Campo, Madrid, Spain
1966	United States	Jack Nicklaus	Arnold Palmer	Tokyo Yomiuri CC, Tokyo, Japan
1967	United States	Jack Nicklaus	Arnold Palmer	Club de Golf Mexico, Mexico City, Mexico
1968	Canada	Al Balding	George Knudson	Circolo Golf Olgiata, Rome, Italy
1969	United States	Lee Trevino	Orville Moody	Singapore Island CC, Singapore
1970	Australia	David Graham	Bruce Devlin	Jockey Club Golf, Buenos Aires, Argentina
1971	United States	Jack Nicklaus	Lee Trevino	PGA National GC, Palm Beach, Florida, USA

The United States and Zimbabwe, winners and runners-up in both 1993 and 1994, walk the final fairway at Dorado Beach. (Opposite) Fred Couples collects the individual prize after his record-breaking performance

1972	Republic of China	Hsieh Min-Nan	Lu Liang-Huan	Royal Melbourne GC, Melbourne, Australia
1973	United States	Johnny Miller	Jack Nicklaus	Golf Nueva Andalucia, Marbella, Spain
1974	South Africa	Bobby Cole	Dale Hayes	Lagunita CC, Caracas, Venezuela
1975	United States	Johnny Miller	Lou Graham	Navatanee GC, Bangkok, Thailand
1976	Spain	Manuel Pinero	Seve Ballesteros	Mission Hills CC, Rancho Mirage, California, USA
1977	Spain	Antonio Garrido	Seve Ballesteros	Wack Wack G & CC, Manila, Philippines
1978	United States	John Mahaffey	Andy North	Princeville Makai GC, Kauai, Hawaii
1979	United States	John Mahaffey	Hale Irwin	Glyfada GC, Athens, Greece
1980	Canada	Dan Halldorson	Jim Nelford	El Rincon Club, Bogota, Columbia
1981	No Tournament			
1982	Spain	Manuel Pinero	José-Maria Canizares	Pierre Marques GC, Acapulco, Mexico
1983	United States	Rex Caldwell	John Cook	Pondok Indah GC, Jakarta, Indonesia
1984	Spain	José-Maria Canizares	Jose Rivero	Olgiata GC, Rome, Italy
1985	Canada	Dave Barr	Dan Halldorson	La Quinta GC, California, USA
1986	No Tournament			
1987	Wales	Ian Woosnam	David Llewellyn	Kapalua Bay GC, Maui, Hawaii
1988	United States	Ben Crenshaw	Mark McCumber	Royal Melbourne GC, Melbourne, Australia
1989	Australia	Peter Fowler	Wayne Grady	Club de Golf Las Brisas, Marbella, Spain
1990	Germany	Bernhard Langer	Torsten Giedeon	Grand Cypress Resort, Florida, USA
1991	Sweden	Per-Ulrik Johansson	Anders Forsbrand	La Querce GC, Rome, Italy
1992	United States	Fred Couples	Davis Love III	La Moraleja, Madrid, Spain
1993	United States	Fred Couples	Davis Love III	Lake Nona, Florida, USA
1994	United States	Fred Couples	Davis Love III	Dorado Beach, Puerto Rico

INTERNATIONAL · TROPHY
(Leading Individual Player)

1953	Antonio Cerda	Argentina
1954	Stan Leonard	Canada
1955	Ed Furgol	United States
1956	Ben Hogan	United States
1957	Torakichi Nakamura	Japan
1958	Angel Miguel	Spain
1959	Stan Leonard	Canada
1960	Flory Van Donck	Belgium
1961	Sam Snead	United States
1962	Roberto de Vicenzo	Argentina
1963	Jack Nicklaus	United States
1964	Jack Nicklaus	United States
1965	Gary Player	South Africa
1966	George Knudson	Canada
1967	Arnold Palmer	United States
1968	Al Balding	Canada
1969	Lee Trevino	United States
1970	Roberto de Vicenzo	Argentina
1971	Jack Nicklaus	United States
1972	Hsieh Min-Nan	Rep. of China
1973	Johnny Miller	United States

1974	Bobby Cole	South Africa
1975	Johnny Miller	United States
1976	Ernesto Acosta	Mexico
1977	Gary Player	South Africa
1978	John Mahaffey	United States
1979	Hale Irwin	United States
1980	Sandy Lyle	Scotland
1981	No Tournament	
1982	Manuel Pinero	Spain
1983	Dave Barr	Canada
1984	José-Maria Canizares	Spain
1985	Howard Clark	England
1986	No Tournament	
1987	Ian Woosnam	Wales
1988	Ben Crenshaw	United States
1989	Peter Fowler	Australia
1990	Payne Stewart	United States
1991	Ian Woosnam	Wales
1992	Brett Ogle	Australia
1993	Bernhard Langer	Germany
1994	Fred Couples	United States

1994 HEINEKEN WORLD CUP GOLF

Dorado Beach, Puerto Rico, November 10 - 13

Couples and Love: alias 'Thunder and Lightning'

Sorry, fellas but the game's up. You cannot fool us anymore. For Couples and Love, now read Thunder and Lightning. This unassuming, laidback image: the 'Dream Team' stuff – it won't wash anymore. Not after what you two did in Puerto Rico. For four days you shoot the lights out, you bring a respectable course to its knees and all you can say is, 'We had a lot of fun out there'! Who are you kidding? You boys are assassins!

It was last November during the 40th staging of the world's oldest international team event that Thunder and Lightning finally blew their cover.

Fred Couples and Davis Love first represented The United States in 1992 at La Moraleja in Spain. They won that tournament on the 72nd green when Love holed a curling, downhill birdie putt to defeat Sweden. A year later at beautiful Lake Nona they went head to head on the final day with the formidable Zimbabwean team of Nick Price and Mark McNulty before eventually pulling away on the back nine to win by five strokes. Only the mighty pairing of Jack Nicklaus and Arnold Palmer had won successive World Cups before. When the Heineken World Cup headed for the lavish Dorado Beach resort on the West Indian island of Puerto Rico, Fred and Davis were determined to make it three in a row.

The United States were drawn to play with the host nation in the opening day's final pairing. Imagine how 16 year old Puerto Rican amateur, Wilfredo Morales must have felt teeing it up with Thunder and Lightning!

He didn't have much time to get nervous, however, as quite early on Thursday the real thing struck... thunder, lightening and an almighty downpour. The lush, tropical vegetation became even more lush and the bunkers threatened to become water hazards. At least the leaderboards made interesting reading during the enforced stoppage: Thailand were in first place (on six under par), followed by Italy and Malaysia. We all wondered if Taipei's Mr Yu and Mr Lu would make an appearance.

When play resumed, reality returned. Couples and Love reeled off a succession of birdies and forced their way to the front. Because of the delay it wasn't possible for the

When the rain stopped, the colours came out. (Left) Wilfredo Morales

last groups to complete their rounds but when they did, early on Friday, the United States were on 12 under par, three ahead of Zimbabwe (McNulty and Johnstone) and five ahead of Italy (Rocca and Grappasonni). Couples had scored a 65, Love a 67. Talk about determined! As for young Morales, he managed a one under par 71, a considerable achievement given the occasion and the auspicious company.

One of the charms of the Heineken World Cup is that in addition to the annual welcoming back of old friends (Bernhard

Langer and Ian Woosnam, for example) each year the tournament unveils a number of less familiar faces. If Morales revelled in the spotlight on Thursday, it was the performance of Malaysia's Marimuthu Ramayah that demanded attention on Friday. Ramayah is no rookie – for one thing he's 39 years old, and he has won his share of tournaments on the Asian Circuit, yet until the second round of the 1994 Heineken World Cup he had never bettered 65. Ramayah scored an excellent 66 on Thursday; now in the second round he played

Malaysia's Marimuthu Ramayah (above) scored eight birdies in a flawless second round 64. (Right) Sweden's Jesper Parnevik and Joakim Haeggman

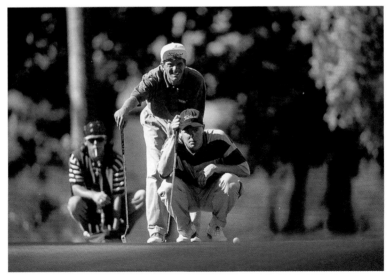

the game of his life, firing eight birdies in a flawless 64. Incredibly, only one of those birdie putts measured more than six feet and he almost holed-in-one at the 8th. 'I've been looking forward to this event all year', he said. Now he'll never forget it.

In normal circumstances Ramayah would have enjoyed a handsome lead in the 'tournament within a tournament', the competition for the International Trophy awarded to the leading individual performer. The problem for Ramayah was that Fred

Couples was playing, if not the best golf of his life, certainly his best golf of the year: Couples added a nine under par 63 to his opening 65. It was scintillating golf. The American made four birdies on the front nine then started back, birdie-birdie-par. The 13th at Dorado Beach is a magnificent dog-legging par five where the approach is played directly towards the ocean, across a lake to a narrow green framed by palm trees. Here, Couples holed a bunker shot for an eagle three. 'Can I hit the ball better? Sure. Can I score better? probably not.'

Canadians Rick Gibson and Dave Barr couldn't repeat their October Dunhill Cup success. (Below) Fred Couples salutes another birdie. After 36 holes the American was 16 under par

With Love adding a none-too-shabby 66 to his opening 67, The United States aggregate total after 36 holes stood at a staggering 27 under par. Who could possibly live with that? Nobody, of course. The amazing Malaysians – Ramayah's partner, Gunasegaran was providing admirable support – were in second position, but they were 11 shots behind the Americans (perhaps they felt they were leading a new

America's honour: Couples and Love cruise to victory

'tournament within a tournament'?) while Sweden (the strong team of Jesper Parnevik and Joakim Haeggman), Italy and Zimbabwe were 13 strokes adrift.

The English – Scottish – Welsh – Irish challenge never materialised at Dorado Beach. After two rounds not one of the British teams figured among the top ten, and only Scotland eventually did (their joint 5th place owing much to a spectacular front nine of 30 on the final day from Gordon Brand Jnr, who had hitherto been outscored by the promising Andrew Coltart, playing in his first World Cup).

Day Three dawned and on a warm, sparkling Saturday Zimbabwe had the temerity to eat into the Americans' lead. Johnstone scored a 66 and McNulty a 67. In fact, their audacity knew no bounds for they then had the cheek to suggest that with the deficit reduced to nine strokes (Couples took 68 and Love 69) the US were still 'catchable'. Everyone else appeared to understand that the queue formed behind Fred and Davis. In any case, Japan were the real stars on Saturday: Masayuki Kawamura and Toru Suzuki scored 65 and 66 respectively to notch the tournament's best one day team score, aside from the Americans' second day heroics. Kawamura's 65 also tied him with Langer for the lowest individual score on Saturday – the German finally showing a glimpse of his best Lake Nona form, where he swept to individual honours. Talking of which, Couples' 68 took him to 20 under par and three ahead of the gallant Ramayah (who would sadly fall away on the final day).

Sunday, then, was destined to be US glory day. Zimbabwe's challenge was never permitted to gain any momentum: Couples struck first with a birdie at the 3rd and both Americans birdied the 4th – the old one-two from Thunder and Lightning. The victory march began as Zimbabwe battled to hold on to second place from a charging Sweden and New Zealand.

Of course, Couples and Love, in keeping with the spirit and traditions of the Heineken World Cup, had to devise a dramatic ending. This being the 40th tournament it was only proper that the winners finished in a record 40 under par and with a winning margin that matched the best of Hogan and Snead (14 strokes at Wentworth in 1956). They were 40 under par playing the final hole but Couples contrived to make his first bogey of the day – not that this affected his winning the International Trophy with a record total but it meant that his partner must make a birdie to ensure that the appropriate figures were achieved. Suddenly… Horror of horrors! Love leaves his approach 70 feet short of the flag. Dramatically… Putt of putts: Love, the longest hitter in the tournament rolls in the longest putt of the week. The legend of Thunder and Lightning lives on.

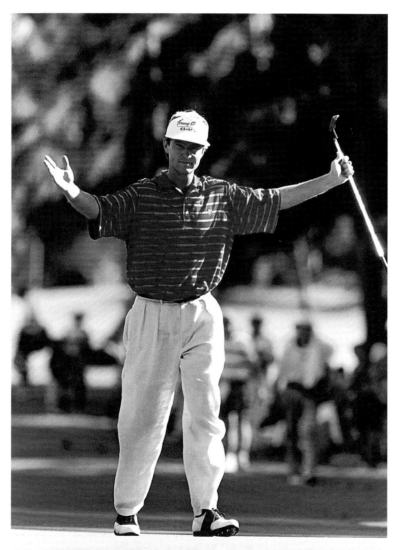

Finishing in style: Davis Love birdies the 72nd hole and the United States finish on 40 under par

1994 Heineken World Cup Golf

Final · Scores

USA	(536)					
Fred Couples	65	63	68	69	265	
Davis Love III	67	66	69	69	271	$150,000 each
Zimbabwe	(550)					
Mark McNulty	68	67	67	70	272	
Tony Johnstone	67	72	66	73	278	75,000 each
Sweden	(551)					
Jesper Parnevik	69	69	70	67	275	
Joakim Haeggman	71	65	70	70	276	50,000 each
New Zealand	(553)					
Frank Nobilo	70	66	67	69	272	
Greg Turner	72	70	68	71	281	37,500 each
Scotland	(557)					
Gordon Brand Jnr	73	69	72	65	279	
Andrew Coltart	71	68	69	70	278	22,833 each
Paraguay	(557)					
Pedro R. Martinez	71	69	69	69	278	
Angel U. Franco	69	68	72	70	279	22,833 each
Japan	(557)					
Masayuki Kawamura	71	67	65	73	276	
Toru Suzuki	75	69	66	72	281	22,833 each
Germany	(558)					
Bernhard Langer	71	71	65	69	276	
Sven Struver	71	69	73	69	282	12,000 each

Australia	(559)					
Steve Elkington	69	68	71	66	274	
Mike Clayton	75	65	75	70	285	9,000 each
Italy	(559)					
Costantino Rocca	68	66	68	68	270	
Silvio Grappasonni	69	71	75	74	289	9,000 each
Malaysia	(559)					
P Gunasegaran	73	69	71	73	286	
Marimuthu Ramayah	66	64	69	74	273	9,000 each
Argentina	(560)					
Eduardo Romero	72	66	66	70	274	
Miguel A Guzman	72	70	73	71	286	7,000 each
Mexico	(563)					
Esteban Toledo	69	72	69	68	278	
Rafael Alarcon	73	73	70	69	285	6,000 each
Canada	(565)					
Dave Barr	72	68	71	72	283	
Rick Gibson	71	66	71	74	282	5,500 each
France	(568)					
Michel Besanceney	74	71	75	69	289	
Jean Van de Velde	73	67	68	71	279	4,350 each
South Africa	(568)					
Roger Wessels	70	68	74	70	282	
Wayne Westner	70	72	73	71	286	4,350 each
Ireland	(568)					
Darren Clarke	69	70	76	71	286	
Paul McGinley	69	70	72	71	282	4,350 each
England	(568)					
Mark Roe	69	71	72	72	284	
Barry Lane	72	70	68	74	284	4,350 each
Korea	(570)					
Young-Keun Han	75	72	68	72	287	
Sang Ho Choi	74	66	72	71	283	3,700 each
Holland	(570)					
Chris Van der Velde	71	71	70	71	283	
Joost Steenkammer	73	67	74	73	287	3,700 each
Thailand	(570)					
Prayad Marksaeng	69	71	67	75	282	
Boonchu Ruangkit	70	71	75	72	288	3,700 each
Brazil	(577)					
Acacio Jorge Pedro	77	70	73	75	295	
Antonio Barcellos	69	68	70	75	288	3,700 each
Finland	(578)					
Mikael Piltz	72	74	67	71	284	
Anssi Kankkonen	72	75	73	74	294	3,350 each

Frank Nobilo and Greg Turner achieved fourth place for New Zealand

Denmark	(578)					
Jacob Rasmussen	78	70	69	75	292	
Steen Tinning	71	73	70	72	286	3,350 each
Wales	(579)					
Phillip Price	77	72	72	81	302	
Ian Woosnam	73	69	66	69	277	3,200 each
Chinese Taipei	(581)					
Yu Chin-Han	75	66	73	74	288	
Lu Chien-Soon	72	73	73	75	293	3,100 each
Spain	(583)					
Jose Rivero	73	71	74	78	296	
Miguel Angel Jimenez	73	70	74	70	287	3,000 each
Switzerland	(592)					
Andre Bossert	71	71	70	73	285	
Marco Scopetta	72	81	72	82	307	2,900 each
Puerto Rico	(595)					
Wilfredo Morales	71	74	72	74	291	
Manuel Camacho	75	73	78	78	304	2,800 each
Hong Kong	(598)					
Richard Kan	79	74	77	74	304	
Dominique Boulet	78	76	67	73	294	2,700 each
Norway	(624)					
Hans Strom-Olsen	84	84	76	80	324	
Thomas Nielsen	76	71	79	74	300	2,600 each
Jamaica	(Disq)					
Ralph Mairs	77	77	77	79	310	2,500 each
Seymour Rose	disq					

LEADING INDIVIDUAL SCORES

F Couples	65	63	68	69	265	$100,000
C Rocca	68	66	68	68	270	50,000
D Love III	67	66	69	69	271	25,000
F Nobilo	70	66	67	69	272	7,500
M McNulty	68	67	67	70	272	7,500
M Ramayah	66	64	69	74	273	
S Elkington	69	68	71	66	274	
E Romero	72	66	66	70	274	
J Parnevik	69	69	70	67	275	
B Langer	71	71	65	69	276	
J Haeggman	71	65	70	70	276	
M Kawamura	71	67	65	73	276	
I Woosnam	73	69	66	69	277	
E Toledo	69	72	69	68	278	
A Coltart	71	68	69	70	278	
P R Martinez	71	69	69	69	278	
T Johnstone	67	72	66	73	278	
J Van de Velde	73	67	68	71	279	
G Brand Jnr	73	69	72	65	279	
A U Franco	69	68	72	70	279	
G Turner	72	70	68	71	281	
T Suzuki	75	68	66	72	281	
A Barcellos	69	68	70	75	282	
R Wessels	70	68	74	70	282	
P McGinley	69	70	72	71	282	

A familiar scene: Davis Love and Fred Couples win their third successive Heineken World Cup

4

GLOBAL GOLF

EUROPE

UNITED STATES

AUSTRALASIA

JAPAN

SOUTH AFRICA

REST OF THE WORLD

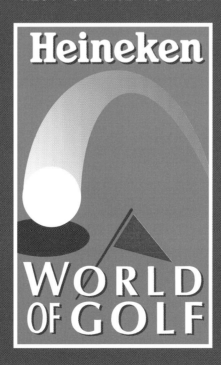

Heineken

WORLD
OF GOLF

EUROPE

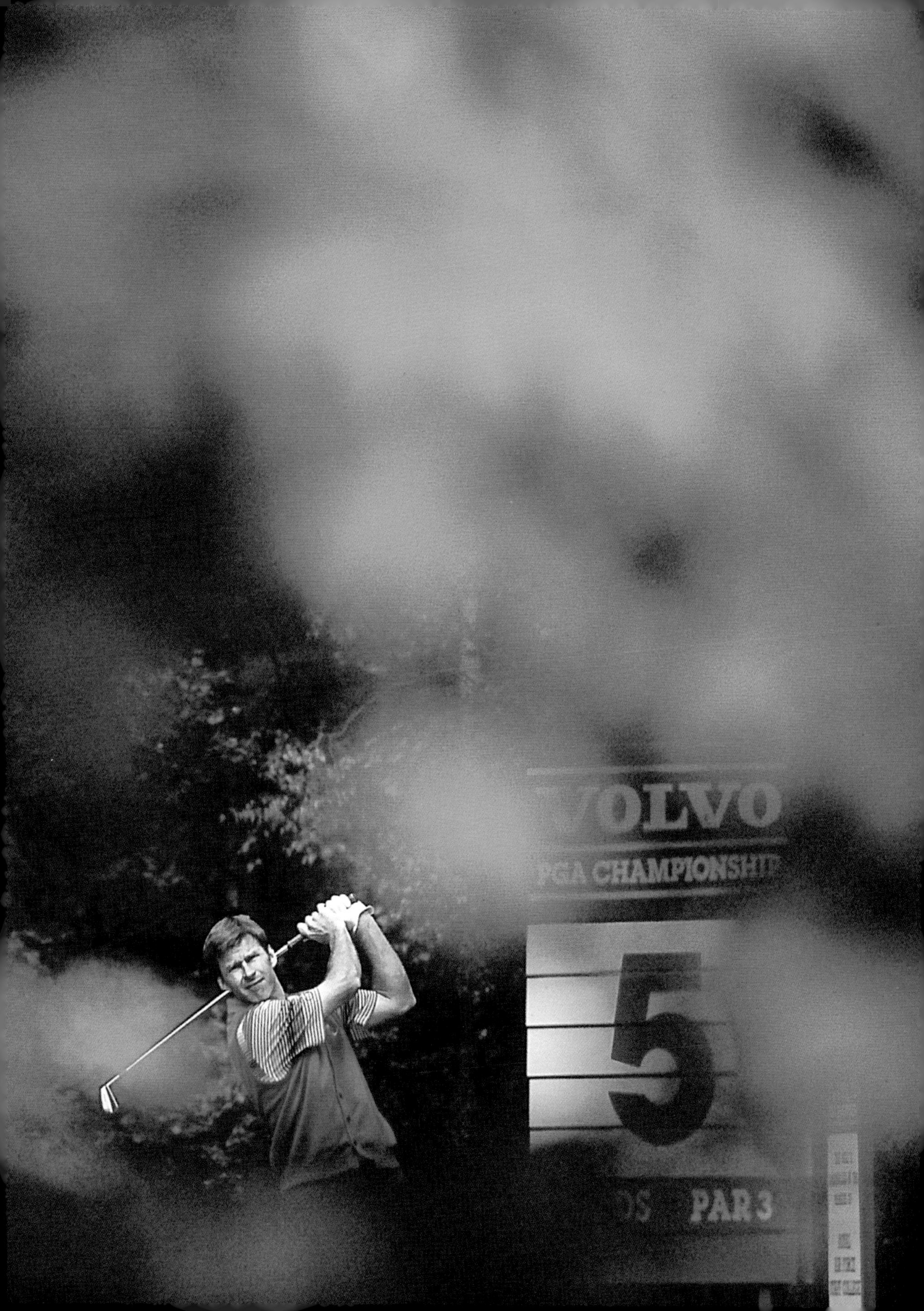
VOLVO
PGA CHAMPIONSHIP
5
PAR 3

1994 PGA EUROPEAN TOUR REVIEW

It was the year the 'old firm' clashed with the 'young guns':

hegemony was at stake

Towards the end of last summer the future of golf – or at least the future of golf in Europe, seemed crystal clear. The halcyon days of Ballesteros, Langer, Faldo and Woosnam were over and the age of Olazabal, Montgomerie, Els (whenever he played in Europe) and the Swedes had begun. At the time – let's say, mid-September, nothing appeared more certain.

Olazabal had captured The Masters and World Series in America in addition to the PGA Championship at Wentworth in a manner reminiscent of Ballesteros in his prime. Meanwhile Seve's much heralded 'return' at St Mellion in May was beginning to look a little hollow – a mere magical blip. The week after St Mellion it was Colin Montgomerie, not Seve, who won the Spanish Open.

What of Ian Woosnam, 'the Welsh Dragon'? Where was the legendary fire and passion? Woosie hadn't featured prominently in any event since the Spring; in June he missed the cut at the US Open, in July the same happened at the British Open and in August Montgomerie relieved him of his English Open title.

Bernhard Langer? Victory in the Irish Open aside, 1994 was proving to be a disappointing year by his imperious standards. For one thing, Langer failed to win the tournament he 'always' wins, the German Open; instead, the winner was... yes, good old Monty.

And Nick Faldo? A sad and disillusioned man in September: at odds with his game and at odds with the media. In fact, throughout the summer, Monty had looked more like his mentor, Faldo, than Faldo himself. In addition to winning the Spanish, English and German Open titles, the Scotsman came close to winning the US Open at Oakmont – losing to Els in a play-off – on the course we all thought was tailor-made for Faldo's game.

Burned out superstars? Yes, crystal clear: a new golfing order was in place; a new era had begun... We should have known better!

(Opposite page) the flying Scotsman: Colin Montgomerie claimed three national open titles during a hugely successful campaign. If the summer belonged to Montgomerie, then the spring belonged the Masters champion, José-Maria Olazabal (right)

What happened after mid-September not only shattered the theory but ensured that 1994 would go down as a vintage year. It wasn't a case of the 'young guns' stumbling in sight of the finishing tape - Montgomerie went on to top the Volvo Order of Merit with record winnings for the season and he and Els contested the World Matchplay final — but the way the 'old firm' came roaring back late in the year which was something truly special.

neat since it was the same margin by which he would claim the final event of the year in Jamaica.

Never one to be overshadowed for long, Dubai runner-up Greg Norman exacted revenge a week later in Thailand when he captured the Johnnie Walker Classic in true Greg Norman style. Who else could roll up complaining of a lung infection, skip all practice, score a 75 on the first day (to be nine strokes behind

Swedish 'young guns'! (Left) Anders Forsbrand; (centre) Robert 'James Dean' Karlsson and (right) Per-Ulrik Johansson

The seeds for a memorable season were sown back in January. The Tour commenced on the island of Madeira, after which it anchored in such classic European ports as Morocco, Dubai and Phuket, Thailand. Swedish golfers won the first two events and looked set to monopolise the early season schedule before Ernie Els went berserk in Dubai. If this was the giant South African's way of preparing us for what lay in store, he couldn't have chosen a more impressive location nor more auspicious company.

Greg Norman and Fred Couples were playing at The Emirates as, of course, were the cream of the European Tour, but it was Els who stole the show, shooting an incredible course record 61 (11 under par) on the opening day. He went on to win the tournament by six strokes, which was rather

Couples), scrape through to the weekend with a second round 70, then score 64-68 finishing with a birdie on the final green to win by one? It was pure theatre and the headline writers were enjoying a golden spell: first the 'Desert Storm' now the 'Shark Attack'.

Peace returned to the Tour as it headed back to the Old World and Messrs Norman and Couples jetted home to America. Indeed, tranquillity reigned, by and large, for the next three months as a mild winter gave way to a warm spring in southern Europe. In Spain, Portugal and France it was the turn of less familiar faces to make an impression.

David Gilford, 'the quiet man of the European Tour' gained the first of his two successes in 1994 in Tenerife and Phillip Price won his first tournament in five years in Portugal. Paul Eales, Stephen Ames and Jose

Coceres each gained their first Tour victories. So, finally, did 40 year old Carl Mason: 'For 21 years I have dreamed of this moment', he said, 'And now it has arrived I cannot think of anything to say.'

Happily for Mason, the prize giving ceremony at the Turespana Masters proved merely a dress rehearsal for his great summer triumph at Gleneagles in the Scottish Open.

Gleneagles seemed a long way off, however, when the Volvo Tour arrived at breezy St Mellion in May. All the pre-tournament talk centred on Olazabal, the new Masters champion, but by the end of the week all eyes were on Seve. Perhaps it was appropriate that the 37 year old's first victory in two years should occur at arguably Europe's toughest venue and on a course designed by Jack Nicklaus – it proves that the atmosphere at St Mellion can be inspiring as well as invigorating. Two new faces also made their mark that week: Gary Orr, the 1993 Rookie of the Year and Jonathan Lomas (who would succeed him in winning that award) tied for third place behind Ballesteros and the fast-finishing Faldo.

But the Summer didn't belong to Seve (nor to Faldo). Montgomerie was the name that always seemed to appear on the final day leaderboards. Of course, he couldn't win every week, in fact, Nick Price won more frequently in America than Monty did in Europe, but it is hard to dispute the contention that the most consistent golfer in the world last year was Colin Montgomerie. And while Ernie Els' ascent to the summit of world golf may have occurred more rapidly, Monty's rise has been inexorable nonetheless. Since he turned professional in 1987, his position on the European Order of Merit makes interesting reading: in 1988 he finished 52nd; in 1989, 25th; in 1990, 14th; in 1991, 4th; in 1992, 3rd; in 1993, 1st and in 1994, 1st again.

In the weeks that followed Montgomerie's

(Top) A reflective Carl Mason. (Above) Early season Tour winners, David Gilford and Paul Eales

victory in the Spanish Open, the parade of Tour winners became very cosmopolitan. Argentina's Eduardo Romero triumphed in Italy and Switzerland; Robert Allenby flew the Australian flag in Germany; Fijian Vijay Singh succeeded

Scotland's Gary Orr: the next Colin Montgomerie? 1993's Rookie of the Year impressed everyone at St Mellion in May during the Benson & Hedges International

in Sweden; Spain's Jimenez won in Holland; England's Faldo and Roe claimed tournaments in Belgium and France and a certain Zimbabwean produced an extraordinary finale to the Open in Scotland.

Some of the season's most exciting finishes also involved an array of international stars. At Mount Juliet in the Murphy's Irish Open, 'special guest' John Daly launched a final round birdie assault to overhaul everyone except Bernhard Langer. The American's score of 65 matched Nick Faldo's course record. In the Volvo PGA Championship at Wentworth Olazabal also produced a closing 65, which on this occasion did prove sufficient to gain him a thrilling one stroke victory over Ernie Els. (Els, of course, gained revenge at the World Matchplay in October, see ahead). Each of these

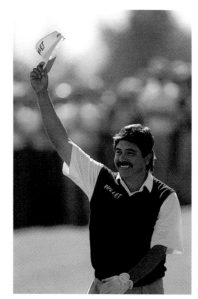

Ian Woosnam was 14 under par for his final 36 holes at Woburn. (Far right) Eduardo Romero wins the European Masters at Crans -sur- Sierre

achievements was impressive, but from mid-September, when the 'old firm' got into its stride they appeared modest by comparison. Was it the performances of the 'young guns' that spurred them into action? Or perhaps the prospect of accumulating a stash of Ryder Cup points for the 1995 contest at Oak Hill? Who knows, but suddenly Seve was scoring 65s like they were going out of fashion; Woosnam was

shooting a 63 to storm home at Woburn and Langer was going one better with an amazing 62 at Valderrama! Nick Faldo couldn't regain his form in time to turn around his European campaign but soon after its completion he too was firing a 63 (in Bali) and ended 1994 by winning a million dollars in South Africa and a further quarter of a million in Jamaica.

Seve's run of form was the most impressive

Where there's a will there's a way. Seve was up to his old tricks in 1994

of all. He came 2nd to Woosnam in the Dunhill British Masters; 3rd to Vijay Singh in the Lancome Trophy, then snatched an improbable win in the German Masters, when he came from three behind Olazabal and six behind Els (the South African had started 63-64) to defeat them both with a birdie at the first sudden death hole. Never mind the Desert Storm and the Shark Attack! Nor had he finished either, for he produced some

(Left) Bernhard Langer breaks the course record with an astonishing 62 at Valderrama. (Above) Stymied! Seve's appeal for relief was refused

superlative golf at the World Matchplay, before losing bravely to the eventual winner, Els and came within a tree trunk (or was it a rabbit dropping?) of winning the Volvo Masters.

But Seve couldn't stop Langer at Valderrama, just as Langer (and the rest) couldn't catch Montgomerie in the Order of Merit. Where was Monty when Seve, Woosie and Langer were weaving their autumnal magic? Right up there on the leaderboard, of course. the burly Scot finished 3rd at Woburn, 4th in Paris, 2nd in the Matchplay and 4th at Valderrama. Whenever you turned and wherever you faced he was there, stalking. You could run from Monty in 1994 but you could never hide.

THE 1994 HEINEKEN DUTCH OPEN

Y ou closed your eyes at Hilversum and for a fleeting moment it was just like old times.... Howard Clark shoots a final round 67 and only one player can catch him, and that man, of course, is Spanish. He needs to make two birdies in his last four holes to tie – or three to win. A twenty-footer disappears at the 15th; the par five 16th yields another birdie and with the 18th also a par five reachable with two goods blows, suddenly it is possible. The final tee shot is not ideal, however, and the approach is hooked wildly almost into the grandstand (typical, you think!) but a deft pitch to six feet and a courageous putt follow and the Spaniard punches the air in celebration of a famous victory.... Then you opened your eyes and you realised that the Spaniard was Miguel Angel Jimenez.

Well, Seve was at Hilversum in July 1994 but when you consider who the pre-tournament favourites were, you appreciate just how much times have changed. Ernie Els, the new US Open champion was present, as was José-Maria Olazabal, the winner of The Masters and, of course, the defending Heineken Dutch Open champion, Colin Montgomerie. Where were Ernie, Ollie and Monty when Messrs Clark and Ballesteros were in their prime?! And where was 30 year old Jimenez?

The weather last July was glorious and the early scoring reflected the mood. Els and Olazabal commenced with matching rounds of 70-66 to be eight under par after 36 holes, yet found themselves four behind surprise leader Peter Mitchell. Jimenez, Montgomerie and David Gilford were just one stroke off the pace

Newly crowned US Open champion, Ernie Els was one of the star attractions at Hilversum last July

**Malaga magic!
Spaniard Miguel
Angel Jimenez
birdies the final
hole – then
celebrates
in style**

and Clark was two behind Mitchell.

Actually, it was too hot. The sun had scorched the fairways to such an extent that by the weekend Hilversum was starting to play more like a golf links than a parkland course. Many among the large galleries expected the conditions to favour Montgomerie but the big Scot stumbled to a 73 on Saturday – a round that effectively dashed his hopes of retaining the title. With Olazabal scoring a modest 72, surely the door was open for Els to chase the leaders? The US Open champion produced a fine 68 in the third round but, again, it wasn't sufficient as Jimenez fired a brilliant 67, courtesy of six birdies and an eagle.

The Spaniard began the final day two strokes clear of Mitchell, three ahead of Clark and four ahead of Els and Gilford. Of the challengers only Clark was able to find his putting touch on Sunday. With a birdie-eagle-birdie burst from the 4th, the Yorkshireman threw down the gauntlet. For a while it looked as if Jimenez might capitulate but then, as he entered the closing stretch, the man from Malaga was able to conjure up the kind of finish that we have long associated with a certain man from Pedrena.

21st - 24th July
HEINEKEN DUTCH OPEN
HILVERSUM

Miguel Angel Jimenez	65	68	67	70	270	£108330
Howard Clark	67	67	71	67	272	72210
Peter Mitchell	65	67	70	71	273	40690
Colin Montgomerie	68	65	73	68	274	27593
John Huston	70	69	67	68	274	27593
David Gilford	66	67	71	70	274	27593
Bradley Hughes	68	71	68	68	275	16753
Ernie Els	70	66	68	71	275	16753
Mark Roe	68	70	69	68	275	16753
Frank Nobilo	69	66	73	68	276	11308
Richard Boxall	65	75	67	69	276	11308
Derrick Cooper	71	67	71	67	276	11308
Eduardo Romero	71	70	66	69	276	11308
Peter O'Malley	71	70	69	66	276	11308
Mike Harwood	70	69	68	70	277	8343
Russell Claydon	67	74	69	67	277	8343
Ruben Alvarez	71	67	69	70	277	8343
Sam Torrance	72	68	69	68	277	8343
Andrew Sherborne	68	75	70	64	277	8343
Paul McGinley	69	71	66	71	277	8343
Philip Walton	69	66	71	71	277	8343
Jamie Spence	69	68	71	69	277	8343
Ian Woosnam	70	69	70	69	278	7020

Miguel Angel Jimenez succeeds Colin Montgomerie as Heineken Dutch Open champion

1994 PGA EUROPEAN TOUR RESULTS

13th - 16th January
MADEIRA ISLAND OPEN
CAMPO DE GOLFE DA MADEIRA

Mats Lanner	70	67	69	206	£41660
Mathias Gronberg	69	70	69	208	18640
Peter Hedblom	69	69	70	208	18640
Howard Clark	68	67	73	208	18640
Miguel Angel Martin	71	69	71	211	8950
Gabriel Hjertstedt	71	67	73	211	8950
Jeremy Robinson	71	66	74	211	8950

20th - 23rd January
MOROCCAN OPEN
GOLF ROYAL DE AGADIR

Anders Forsbrand	70	68	69	69	276	£58330
Howard Clark	68	67	72	73	280	38880
Robert Karlsson	68	72	70	71	281	21910
Peter Hedblom	68	72	73	69	282	16165
Frank Nobilo	72	72	68	70	282	16165
Jonathan Sewell	68	72	74	69	283	10500
Scott Watson	73	72	68	70	283	10500
Jean Van de Velde	72	68	71	72	283	10500
Andrew Coltart	74	69	75	66	284	7820

27th - 30th January
DUBAI DESERT CLASSIC
EMIRATES GOLF CLUB

Ernie Els	61	69	67	71	268	£75000
Greg Norman	68	69	68	69	274	50000
Wayne Westner	70	68	69	68	275	28170
Jonathan Lomas	66	73	70	67	276	19103
Isao Aoki	67	72	70	67	276	19103
Tsukasa Watanabe	70	70	67	69	276	19103
Per-Ulrik Johansson	70	71	69	67	277	12375
Gary Evans	67	69	71	70	277	12375
Craig Cassells	68	69	69	72	278	9525
Klas Eriksson	69	69	70	70	278	9525

3rd - 6th February
JOHNNIE WALKER CLASSIC
BLUE CANYON CC, PHUKET

Greg Norman	75	70	64	68	277	£100000
Fred Couples	66	72	70	70	278	66660
Bernhard Langer	68	70	71	70	279	37560
Ian Woosnam	68	72	68	73	281	30000
Mike Harwood	71	72	69	70	282	25400
Colin Montgomerie	70	72	71	70	283	19500

Ernie Els is congratulated by Greg Norman after his stunning victory in Dubai

Chin-Sheng Hsieh	70	69	70	74	283	19500
Frankie Minoza	72	74	67	71	284	14220
David Feherty	69	71	73	71	284	14220
Pierre Fulke	74	70	72	69	285	11106
Isao Aoki	70	71	71	73	285	11106
Sven Struver	77	70	69	69	285	11106

10th - 13th February
TURESPANA OPEN DE TENERIFE
GOLF DEL SUR, TENERIFE

David Gilford	72	70	66	70	278	£41660
Wayne Riley	68	71	70	71	280	18640
Andrew Murray	73	67	68	72	280	18640
Juan Quiros	70	68	67	75	280	18640
Bill Malley	69	76	69	67	281	8275
Jose Maria Canizares	67	70	73	71	281	8275
David Ray	70	70	69	72	281	8275
Brian Barnes	73	67	64	77	281	8275

17th - 20th February
OPEN DE EXTREMADURA
GOLF DEL GUADIANA

Paul Eales	72	69	69	71	281	£41660
Peter Hedblom	72	69	71	70	282	27770
Andrew Coltart	68	74	71	70	283	14075
Jose Maria Canizares	70	73	68	72	283	14075
Ian Spencer	74	71	68	71	284	7283
Lee Westwood	68	72	72	72	284	7283
Peter Mitchell	69	69	74	72	284	7283
Jim Payne	72	70	70	72	284	7283
Miguel Angel Jimenez	67	73	69	75	284	7283
Nic Henning	72	71	66	75	284	7283

24th - 27th February
TURESPANA MASTERS OPEN DE ANDALUCIA
MONTECASTILLO GOLF RESORT, JEREZ

Carl Mason	67	70	71	70	278	£50535
José-Maria Olazabal	69	68	71	72	280	33670
Gordon Brand Jnr	71	69	69	72	281	18988
Per-Ulrik Johansson	69	72	71	70	282	15166
Miguel Angel Jimenez	70	73	72	68	283	12861
Ian Palmer	69	71	72	72	284	8523

Jay Townsend	67	74	71	72	284	8523
Peter Teravainen	70	73	68	73	284	8523
Ross Drummond	69	69	73	73	284	8523

3rd - 6th March
TURESPANA OPEN MEDITERRANIA
VILLA MARTIN, TORREVIEJA

*José-Maria Olazabal	70	65	71	70	276	£50000
Paul McGinley	70	68	68	70	276	33330
Peter Baker	73	71	65	69	278	16890
Gordon J Brand	68	66	70	74	278	16890
Klas Eriksson	67	72	70	70	279	10733
Robert Allenby	70	68	71	70	279	10733
Tony Johnstone	68	68	68	75	279	10733
Phil Golding	68	73	70	69	280	7095
Juan Quiros	67	67	71	75	280	7095

10th -13th March
TURESPANA OPEN DE BALEARES
SON VIDA

Barry Lane	64	70	66	69	269	£41616
Jim Payne	67	68	70	66	271	27727
Wayne Westner	68	70	67	68	273	15637
Paul Lawrie	74	65	69	67	275	11540
Lee Westwood	69	67	71	68	275	11540
Sven Struver	71	67	72	67	277	7493
Andrew Coltart	73	69	67	68	277	7493
Jose Rivero	72	67	66	72	277	7493

17th - 20th March
PORTUGUESE OPEN
PENHA LONGA GOLF CLUB

Phillip Price	64	71	71	72	278	£50000
David Gilford	71	69	69	73	282	22370
Retief Goosen	69	66	73	74	282	22370
Paul Eales	66	71	72	73	282	22370
Costantino Rocca	65	73	74	71	283	11600
Ignacio Garrido	69	69	73	72	283	11600
Miguel Angel Jimenez	70	68	74	72	284	8250
Glenn Ralph	71	69	71	73	284	8250

*winner in play-off

1st - 4th April
OPEN V33
TERRAIN DES SANGLIERS, GOLF CLUB DE LYON

Stephen Ames	70	67	71	74	282	£37500
Pedro Linhart	72	68	72	72	284	19535
Gabriel Hjertstedt	68	68	71	77	284	19535
Wayne Riley	69	68	69	79	285	11250
Gary Orr	69	66	76	75	286	9500
Michel Besanceney	69	75	68	75	287	7275
David Gilford	70	73	71	73	287	7275
Phillip Walton	72	71	72	73	288	5030
Gordon J Brand	70	69	73	76	288	5030
Miles Tunnicliff	72	68	75	73	288	5030

14th - 17th April
TOURNOI PERRIER DE PARIS
GOLF DE SAINT-CLOUD

Peter Baker & David J Russell						(each)
	58	68	65	69	260	£35000
Mark Mouland & Jamie Spence						
	62	69	66	64	261	25000
Russell Claydon & Paul Eales						
	60	66	71	66	263	15000
Seve Ballesteros & José-Maria Olazabal						
	63	67	67	66	263	15000
Miguel Angel Jimenez & Jose Rivero						
	66	70	64	64	264	9000
Mark Davis & David Jones						
	66	68	67	64	265	5583
Andrew Sherborne & Paul Curry						
	65	68	67	65	265	5583
Thomas Levet & Marc Pendaries						
	62	71	66	66	265	5583

21st - 24th April
HEINEKEN OPEN CATALONIA
PALS, GIRONA

Jose Coceres	70	69	67	69	275	£50000
Jean Louis Guepy	67	68	72	71	278	33330
Russell Claydon	72	73	69	65	279	18780
Sam Torrance	70	73	70	67	280	15000
Wayne Riley	68	69	74	70	281	9925

Adam Hunter	70	72	69	70	281	9925
Pierre Fulke	71	71	69	70	281	9925
Gordon Brand Jnr	70	72	69	70	281	9925
Mark Mouland	70	72	71	69	282	6690
Ignacio Garrido	74	73	70	66	283	5560
Frank Nobilo	71	68	71	73	283	5560
Retief Goosen	74	65	69	75	283	5560

28th April - 1st May
AIR FRANCE CANNES OPEN
CANNES-MOUGINS

Ian Woosnam	72	70	63	66	271	£50000
Colin Montgomerie	70	69	67	70	276	33330
Jean Van de Velde	73	71	68	65	277	16890
Wayne Riley	69	69	73	66	277	16890
Pierre Fulke	68	69	69	72	278	12700
Terry Price	69	71	70	71	281	12700
Santiago Luna	69	69	76	67	281	7195
Tony Johnstone	69	69	74	69	281	7195
Russell Claydon	72	67	73	69	281	7195
Darren Clarke	69	69	72	71	281	7195
Sam Torrance	65	68	76	72	281	7195
Per-Ulrik Johansson	73	70	69	69	281	7195

The day an Argentinian reigned in Spain: Jose Coceres captured the Heineken Open Catalonia in April. (Opposite page) Fellow countryman, Eduardo Romero claimed the Italian Open

The smile returns: Seve Ballesteros at St Mellion

5th - 8th May
BENSON AND HEDGES INTERNATIONAL OPEN
ST MELLION G & CC, CORNWALL

Seve Ballesteros	69	70	72	70	281	£108330
Nick Faldo	75	69	70	70	284	72210
Jonathan Lomas	74	70	69	72	285	36595
Gary Orr	70	70	70	75	285	36595
Wayne Westner	70	74	69	74	287	20108
Phillip Price	69	73	71	74	287	20108
Robert Karlsson	73	72	70	72	287	20108
Sam Torrance	75	68	69	75	287	20108
Paul Curry	76	69	70	72	287	20108
Alexander Cejka	76	72	67	73	288	11650
Mark Roe	73	72	71	72	288	11650
Howard Clark	70	72	75	71	288	11650
Jose Rivero	70	73	75	70	288	11650

12th - 15th May
PEUGEOT OPEN DE ESPANA
CLUB DE CAMPO, MADRID

Colin Montgomerie	70	71	66	70	277	£83330
Mark Roe	70	68	69	71	278	37283
Richard Boxall	69	69	70	70	278	37283
Mark McNulty	68	69	70	71	278	37283
Bernhard Langer	70	69	69	71	279	21200
Jonathan Lomas	74	73	67	67	281	16250
Ernie Els	67	74	73	67	281	16250
Phillip Price	72	72	67	71	282	9911

Steen Tinning	74	69	71	68	282	9911
Seve Ballesteros	72	71	73	66	282	9911
José-Maria Olazabal	71	70	69	72	282	9911
Gordon Brand Jnr	69	72	71	70	282	9911
Frederic Regard	69	71	71	71	282	9911

19th - 22nd May
TISETTANTA ITALIAN OPEN
MARCO SIMONE, ROME

Eduardo Romero	69	67	69	67	272	£75000
Greg Turner	69	69	70	65	273	50000
Fredrik Lindgren	71	64	69	71	275	28170
Anders Forsbrand	73	69	66	68	276	16412
Peter Teravainen	71	73	65	67	276	16412
Robert Allenby	70	71	69	66	276	16412
Paul Eales	65	70	70	71	276	16412
John Bland	70	67	69	70	276	16412
Robert Lee	71	68	69	69	277	10050

27th - 30th May
VOLVO PGA CHAMPIONSHIP
WENTWORTH CLUB, SURREY

José-Maria Olazabal	67	68	71	65	271	£133330
Ernie Els	66	66	71	69	272	88880
Bernhard Langer	69	70	67	68	274	50070
Joakim Haeggman	69	69	70	68	276	36940
Miguel Angel Jimenez	68	66	72	70	276	36940
Seve Ballesteros	73	66	70	68	277	28000
Mark James	68	72	71	67	278	24000
Adam Hunter	71	65	72	71	279	20000
Sandy Lyle	68	71	70	71	280	17840
Malcolm Mackenzie	73	70	69	69	281	14340
Frank Nobilo	73	66	69	73	281	14340
Peter Hedblom	69	69	71	72	281	14340
Kevin Stables	71	71	71	68	281	14340

2nd - 5th June
ALFRED DUNHILL OPEN
ROYAL ZOUTE GC, KNOKKE, BELGIUM

*Nick Faldo	67	74	67	71	279	£100000
Joakim Haeggman	73	68	66	72	279	66660
Peter Hedblom	69	73	65	73	280	30986
Bernhard Langer	69	68	68	75	280	30986
Colin Montgomerie	67	70	66	77	280	30986
Ignacio Garrido	67	70	71	73	281	19500
Philip Walton	73	67	69	72	281	19500
Mike Clayton	68	70	73	71	282	14220
Andrew Murray	69	71	69	73	282	14220

9th - 12th June
HONDA OPEN
GUT KADEN, HAMBURG, GERMANY

*Robert Allenby	72	67	68	69	276	£83330
Miguel Angel Jimenez	70	71	65	70	276	55550
Rodger Davis	66	68	76	68	278	31300
David Gilford	70	70	68	71	279	25000
Bernhard Langer	70	72	72	66	280	16550
Gabriel Hjertstedt	69	71	73	67	280	16550
Andrew Coltart	69	69	69	73	280	16550
Paul Lawrie	68	71	72	69	280	16550

Masters winner, José-Maria Olazabal completed the Spring double at Wentworth

16th - 19th June
JERSEY EUROPEAN AIRWAYS OPEN
LA MOYE GOLF CLUB, ST BRELADE, JERSEY

Paul Curry	73	62	68	63	266	£58330
Mark James	69	63	68	69	269	38880
Iain Pyman	66	67	68	70	271	21910
Rodger Davis	69	66	66	72	273	13770
Jim Payne	70	69	67	67	273	13770
Peter Mitchell	70	68	66	69	273	13770
Tommy Horton	71	65	70	67	273	13770

23rd - 26th June
PEUGEOT OPEN DE FRANCE
NATIONAL GC, PARIS

Mark Roe	70	71	67	66	274	£91660
Gabriel Hjertstedt	67	70	68	70	275	61100
José-Maria Olazabal	68	72	69	69	278	34430
Lee Westwood	66	74	68	71	279	27500
Andrew Coltart	68	70	71	71	280	19683
Robert Allenby	71	71	71	67	280	19683
Paul McGinley	70	72	67	71	280	19683

30th June - 3rd July
MURPHY'S IRISH OPEN
MOUNT JULIET, THOMASTOWN, CO KILKENNY

Bernhard Langer	70	68	70	67	275	£98765
John Daly	70	68	73	65	276	51466
Robert Allenby	68	68	68	72	276	51466
Greg Turner	73	70	69	66	278	27358
José-Maria Olazabal	68	68	71	71	278	27358
Peter Baker	70	68	71	70	279	19259
Steven Richardson	71	70	69	69	279	19259
Alberto Binaghi	69	70	70	71	280	11369

Mike Harwood	69	69	70	72	280	11369
Paul Moloney	71	70	67	72	280	11369
Ernie Els	71	73	67	69	280	11369
Sam Torrance	65	73	73	69	280	11369
Craig Parry	70	69	70	71	280	11369
Nick Faldo	69	71	67	73	280	11369

6th - 9th July
BELL'S SCOTTISH OPEN
GLENEAGLES HOTEL, PERTHSHIRE

Carl Mason	67	69	61	68	265	£100000
Peter Mitchell	67	64	65	70	266	66660
Jesper Parnevik	70	65	64	68	267	37560
Colin Montgomerie	67	66	69	66	268	30000
Darren Clarke	67	67	67	69	270	23200
Jonathan Lomas	66	66	68	70	270	23200
Andrew Oldcorn	70	63	67	71	271	13892
Jim McGovern	71	65	68	67	271	13892
Miguel Angel Martin	70	65	65	71	271	13892
Brett Ogle	72	66	66	67	271	13892

14th - 17th July
THE OPEN CHAMPIONSHIP
TURNBERRY, AYRSHIRE

(See page 59)

21st - 24th July
HEINEKEN DUTCH OPEN
HILVERSUM

(See page 99)

Grey skies, 65. John Daly charged through the field on the final day at Mount Juliet

28th - 31st July
SCANDINAVIAN MASTERS
DROTTNINGHOLM GC, STOCKHOLM, SWEDEN

Vijay Singh	68	67	69	64	268	£108330
Mark McNulty	67	69	69	66	271	72210
Per Haugsrud	70	66	68	68	272	33573
Jesper Parnevik	69	71	65	67	272	33573
Mark Davis	64	72	65	71	272	33573
Mark Roe	66	72	64	71	273	22750
Robert Karlsson	70	68	69	67	274	17875
Sven Struver	70	65	70	69	274	17875

4th - 7th August
BMW INTERNATIONAL OPEN
ST EURACH LAND-UND GC, MUNICH

Mark McNulty	70	71	68	65	274	£87500
Seve Ballesteros	69	68	72	66	275	58250
Mark Roe	68	71	68	69	276	32750
Darren Clarke	67	69	68	73	277	26200
John Bland	71	72	67	68	278	20250
Jeremy Robinson	67	71	71	69	278	20250
Derrick Cooper	72	69	70	68	279	11147
Jeff Hawkes	71	70	71	67	279	11147
Niclas Fasth	67	73	68	71	279	11147
Ross McFarlane	72	68	66	73	279	11147
Costantino Rocca	73	71	70	65	279	11147
Peter Mitchell	73	66	68	72	279	11147
Sven Struver	73	70	67	69	279	11147

11th - 14th August
HOHE BRUCKE OPEN
GC WALDVIERTEL, LITSCHAU, AUSTRIA

Mark Davis	68	69	69	64	270	£41660
Philip Walton	68	65	69	70	272	27770
Retief Goosen	68	72	66	67	273	15650
Andrew Coltart	72	69	68	66	275	10616
Michel Besanceney	69	68	69	69	275	10616
Andrew Sherborne	73	65	66	71	275	10616
Paul Mayo	71	68	69	69	277	6875
Heinz P Thul	69	69	69	70	277	6875

*winner in play-off

18th - 21st August
MURPHY'S ENGLISH OPEN
FOREST OF ARDEN HOTEL & CC, WARWICKSHIRE

Colin Montgomerie	70	67	68	69	274	£100000
Barry Lane	66	69	72	68	275	66660
Retief Goosen	72	72	65	67	276	37560
Gordon Brand Jnr	69	70	70	68	277	27700
Des Smyth	69	68	66	74	277	27700
Mark Davis	72	70	66	71	279	18000
Costantino Rocca	67	69	72	71	279	18000
Andre Bossert	69	71	69	70	279	18000
Sam Torrance	70	69	72	70	281	13440

25th - 28th August
VOLVO GERMAN OPEN
HUBBELRATH, DUSSELDORF

Colin Montgomerie	65	68	66	70	269	£108330
Bernhard Langer	69	68	65	68	270	72210
Phillip Price	65	67	67	72	271	40690
Per-Ulrik Johansson	64	70	70	68	272	30015
Ross McFarlane	68	65	67	72	272	30015
Thomas Levet	63	72	67	71	273	21125
Miguel Angel Jimenez	69	71	65	68	273	21125
Gordon Brand Jnr	67	68	72	67	274	16250
Vicente Fernandez	70	67	70	69	276	14510
Mike Clayton	71	68	70	68	277	13000

1st - 4th September
CANON EUROPEAN MASTERS
CRANS-SUR-SIERRE, SWITZERLAND

Eduardo Romero	64	68	66	68	266	£111290
Pierre Fulke	70	65	65	67	267	74150
Jean Van De Velde	68	68	67	66	269	34513
Barry Lane	67	68	66	67	269	34513
Sam Torrance	67	65	69	68	269	34513
Nick Faldo	69	66	67	68	270	21710
Martin Gates	69	65	70	66	270	21710
Bernhard Langer	69	70	64	68	271	15830
Adam Hunter	65	69	68	69	271	15830
Per-Ulrik Johansson	69	68	67	68	272	12380
Retief Goosen	68	69	67	68	272	12380
Gordon Brand Jnr	65	65	71	71	272	12380

8th - 11th September
EUROPEAN OPEN CHAMPIONSHIP
EAST SUSSEX NATIONAL, UCKFIELD

David Gilford	70	68	70	67	275	£100000
Costantino Rocca	68	72	70	70	280	52110
José-Maria Olazabal	68	74	69	69	280	52110
Colin Montgomerie	66	73	73	70	282	30000
Howard Clark	71	68	74	71	284	21466
Darren Clarke	71	74	71	68	284	21466
Craig Cassells	72	73	69	70	284	21466
Seve Ballesteros	68	75	72	70	285	15000

15th - 18th September
DUNHILL BRITISH MASTERS
WOBURN G & CC, BUCKS

Ian Woosnam	71	70	63	67	271	£108330
Seve Ballesteros	69	65	69	72	275	72210
Colin Montgomerie	72	66	70	68	276	36595
Bernhard Langer	71	69	65	71	276	36595
Ernie Els	68	71	70	68	277	25140
Jose Rivero	74	67	68	68	277	25140
Eoghan O'Connell	71	69	70	68	278	16753
Philip Walton	68	72	66	72	278	16753
Miguel Angel Martin	71	69	65	73	278	16753
Martin Gates	67	70	72	70	279	12046
Andrew Murray	67	69	72	71	279	12046
Sam Torrance	70	70	68	71	279	12046

Colin Montgomerie adopts a familiar pose at the Murphy's English Open

22nd - 25th September
TROPHEE LANCOME
ST NOM LA BRETECHE, PARIS

Vijay Singh	65	63	69	66	263	£100000
Miguel Angel Jimenez	67	64	66	67	264	66000
Seve Ballesteros	65	69	66	65	265	37000
Colin Montgomerie	69	66	67	68	270	30000
José-Maria Olazabal	68	68	71	65	272	23000
Barry Lane	71	68	66	67	272	23000
Nick Faldo	68	71	66	68	273	15350
Mark Davis	69	66	67	71	273	15350

30th September - 3rd October
MERCEDES GERMAN MASTERS
MOTZENER SEE G&CC, BERLIN

*Seve Ballesteros	68	70	65	67	270	£104,125
Ernie Els	63	64	70	73	270	54,250
José-Maria Olazabal	67	67	66	70	270	54,250
Vijay Singh	66	70	70	67	273	24,593
Nick Faldo	69	68	67	69	273	24,593
Sven Struver	67	70	70	66	273	24,593
Eamonn Darcy	70	69	66	68	273	24,593
Peter Mitchell	66	70	68	70	274	14,812

6th - 9th October
ALFRED DUNHILL CUP
THE OLD COURSE, ST ANDREWS

Semi-Finals
USA bt ENGLAND 3 - 0
Kite (69) bt Roe (70)   Couples (68) bt Clark (74)
Strange (70) bt Lane (71)
CANADA bt SOUTH AFRICA 2 - 1
Stewart (70) bt Frost (75)   Gibson (70) bt Westner (74)
Barr (72) lost to Els (68)
England and South Africa received £31,666 per man

Final
CANADA bt USA 2 - 1
Barr (70) bt Kite (71)   Gibson (74) lost to Strange (67)
Stewart (71) bt Couples (72)
Canada received £100,000 per man, USA £50,000 per man

20th - 23rd October
CHEMAPOL TROPHY CZECH OPEN
MARIANSKE LAZNE GC, CZECH REPUBLIC

Per-Ulrik Johansson	61	56	54	66	237	£83330
Klas Eriksson	59	58	56	67	240	55550
Russell Claydon	56	61	57	67	241	28150
Frank Nobilo	54	59	57	71	241	28150
Sven Struver	58	58	54	72	242	15470
Joakim Haeggman	59	55	60	68	242	15470
Darren Clarke	59	56	57	70	242	15470
Jose Rivero	59	57	56	70	242	15470

27th - 30th October
VOLVO MASTERS
VALDERRAMA, SOTOGRANDE, SPAIN

Bernhard Langer	71	62	73	70	276	£125000
Vijay Singh	71	70	70	66	277	65175
Seve Ballesteros	69	67	68	73	277	65175
Miguel Angel Jimenez	65	70	72	71	278	34800
Colin Montgomerie	69	65	72	72	278	34800
Mark McNulty	70	69	69	71	279	26800
Costantino Rocca	69	72	67	73	281	23000
Ian Woosnam	68	69	73	72	282	18250
José-Maria Olazabal	70	70	71	71	282	18250
Frank Nobilo	70	69	73	71	283	15500

*winner in play-off

Canada surprised the US and the world at St Andrews

1994 PGA EUROPEAN TOUR WINNERS SUMMARY

TOURNAMENT · WINNERS

January

MADEIRA ISLAND OPEN	Mats Lanner	(Swe)
MOROCCAN OPEN	Anders Forsbrand	(Swe)
DUBAI DESERT CLASSIC	Ernie Els	(SA)

February

JOHNNIE WALKER CLASSIC	Greg Norman	(Aus)
TURESPANA OPEN DE TENERIFE	David Gilford	(Eng)
OPEN DE EXTREMADURA	Paul Eales	(Eng)
TURESPANA MASTERS OPEN DE ANDALUCIA	Carl Mason	(Eng)

March

TURESPANA OPEN MEDITERRANIA	José-Maria Olazabal	(Sp)
TURESPANA OPEN DE BALEARES	Barry Lane	(Eng)
PORTUGUESE OPEN	Phillip Price	(Wal)

April

OPEN V33	Stephen Ames	(T&T)
TOURNOI PERRIER DE PARIS	Peter Baker	(Eng)
	& David J Russell	(Eng)
HEINEKEN OPEN CATALONIA	Jose Coceres	(Arg)
AIR FRANCE CANNES OPEN	Ian Woosnam	(Wal)

May

BENSON & HEDGES INTERNATIONAL OPEN	Seve Ballesteros	(Sp)
PEUGEOT OPEN DE ESPANA	Colin Montgomerie	(Scot)
TISETTANTA ITALIAN OPEN	Eduardo Romero	(Arg)
VOLVO PGA CHAMPIONSHIP	José-Maria Olazabal	(Sp)

June

ALFRED DUNHILL OPEN	Nick Faldo	(Eng)
HONDA OPEN	Robert Allenby	(Aus)
JERSEY EUROPEAN AIRWAYS OPEN	Paul Curry	(Eng)
PEUGEOT OPEN DE FRANCE	Mark Roe	(Eng)
MURPHY'S IRISH OPEN	Bernhard Langer	(Ger)

July

BELL'S SCOTTISH OPEN	Carl Mason	(Eng)
123RD OPEN GOLF CHAMPIONSHIP	Nick Price	(Zim)
HEINEKEN DUTCH OPEN	Miguel Angel Jimenez	(Sp)
SCANDINAVIAN MASTERS	Vijay Singh	(Fij)

August

BMW INTERNATIONAL OPEN	Mark McNulty	(Zim)
HOHE BRUCKE OPEN	Mark Davis	(Eng)
MURPHY'S ENGLISH OPEN	Colin Montgomerie	(Scot)
VOLVO GERMAN OPEN	Colin Montgomerie	(Scot)

September

CANON EUROPEAN MASTERS	Eduardo Romero	(Arg)
EUROPEAN OPEN CHAMPIONSHIP	David Gilford	(Eng)
DUNHILL BRITISH MASTERS	Ian Woosnam	(Wal)
TROPHEE LANCOME	Vijay Singh	(Fij)
MERCEDES GERMAN MASTERS	Seve Ballesteros	(Sp)

October

ALFRED DUNHILL CUP	Canada	
TOYOTA WORLD MATCHPLAY CHAMPIONSHIP	Ernie Els	(SA)
CHEMAPOL TROPHY CZECH OPEN	Per-Ulrik Johansson	(Swe)
VOLVO MASTERS	Bernhard Langer	(Ger)

1994 PGA
EUROPEAN TOUR

VOLVO ORDER OF MERIT: TOP 100

Europe's Number One

1	Colin Montgomerie	£762,719				66	Ross McFarlane	84,279
2	Bernhard Langer	635,483				67	Andrew Murray	81,190
3	Seve Ballesteros	590,101				68	Jose Coceres	81,146
4	José-Maria Olazabal	516,107				69	Adam Hunter	80,813
5	Miguel Angel Jimenez	437,403				70	Mats Lanner	79,811
6	Vijay Singh	364,313				71	Silvio Grappasonni	73,407
7	David Gilford	326,629				72	Tony Johnstone	73,278
8	Nick Faldo	321,256				73	Domingo Hospital	73,004
9	Mark Roe	312,539				74	Steven Richardson	72,252
10	Ernie Els	311,849				75	Andre Bossert	72,239
11	Barry Lane	277,362				76	Paul Lawrie	71,975
12	Ian Woosnam	273,264	39	Retief Goosen	140,820	77	David Feherty	71,475
13	Mark McNulty	270,349	40	Gary Orr	138,575	78	Jeremy Robinson	71,300
14	Eduardo Romero	269,422	41	Sven Struver	137,682	79	Santiago Luna	70,912
15	Per-Ulrik Johansson	259,952	42	Andrew Coltart	136,357	80	Michel Besanceney	70,301
16	Howard Clark	247,865	43	Lee Westwood	122,322	81	Peter Teravainen	67,886
17	Robert Allenby	240,174	44	Miguel Angel Martin	121,592	82	Gordon J Brand	67,058
18	Peter Mitchell	231,332	45	Klas Eriksson	121,437	83	Alberto Binaghi	66,735
19	Carl Mason	205,112	46	Paul McGinley	121,020	84	Martin Gates	62,715
20	Frank Nobilo	191,583	47	Jose Rivero	120,723	85	Peter O'Malley	59,723
21	Anders Forsbrand	191,235	48	Rodger Davis	117,262	86	Mathias Gronberg	59,542
22	Sam Torrance	186,043	49	Philip Walton	115,352	87	Gary Evans	59,513
23	Pierre Fulke	178,842	50	Wayne Westner	114,569	88	Thomas Levet	58,375
24	Gordon Brand Jnr	171,602	51	Mike Clayton	110,185	89	Fredrik Lindgren	58,292
25	Joakim Haeggman	170,989	52	Jean Van de Velde	109,067	90	Eoghan O'Connell	58,123
26	Jesper Parnevik	169,633	53	Wayne Riley	107,300	91	Steen Tinning	58,120
27	Greg Turner	168,136	54	Mike Harwood	99,883	92	Jamie Spence	57,283
28	Russell Claydon	167,328	55	Peter Baker	99,660	93	Pedro Linhart	57,164
29	Mark James	166,434	56	Robert Karlsson	98,482	94	Andrew Oldcorn	55,893
30	Costantino Rocca	165,121	57	Richard Boxall	96,521	95	Derrick Cooper	55,674
31	Mark Davis	164,885	58	Stephen Ames	95,905	96	Ross Drummond	54,600
32	Jonathan Lomas	162,715	59	Jim Payne	94,742	97	Malcolm Mackenzie	53,236
33	Paul Curry	161,633	60	Des Smyth	94,090	98	Craig Cassells	53,048
34	Phillip Price	158,756	61	Sandy Lyle	93,695	99	Terry Price	52,614
35	Paul Eales	151,977	62	John Bland	91,499	100	Jay Townsend	51,698
36	Peter Hedblom	151,441	63	Ignacio Garrido	90,088			
37	Darren Clarke	148,685	64	Ronan Rafferty	86,179			
38	Gabriel Hjertstedt	142,805	65	Andrew Sherborne	86,098			

THE WORLD MATCHPLAY CHAMPIONSHIP

by Richard Dyson

Wentworth in Autumn and Seve Ballesteros have had a love affair stretching back to 1976, so when the 12-man line-up for the 1994 World Matchplay was announced, and to general horror, excluded the Spaniard, there was little wonder that this proud and passionate man felt jilted. True, he had cut a sad figure after his first round 7 & 6 thrashing by David Frost in 1993, when he, himself, raised doubts about his return to the championship he has claimed a joint-record five times. However, Seve in 1994 was rejuvenated and back to winning ways; to deny him his 19th consecutive appearance in the event, before his adoring British public, seemed to many, to be nothing short of sacrilege. Normally, the withdrawal of crowd-pulling John Daly would have been greeted with some dismay but on this occasion it was widely greeted with joy – Seve was in after all – if only by the 'tradesman's entrance'.

Ballesteros' presence (along with Faldo, Woosnam and defending champion Pavin) meant that the field for the 31st World Matchplay could boast four former winners, indeed, all four champions so far in the 1990s. Though the likes of Price, Norman, Langer and Couples were absent, it was still a high class entry, with a blend of youth and experience.

The immovable object: Seve Ballesteros was back and gunning for a record sixth World Matchplay title

Smiles all round: José-Maria Olazabal and Ernie Els during their semi-final encounter at Wentworth

Thursday at Wentworth was one of those golfing days that live long in the memory. The immaculately conditioned West Course looked a picture in its glorious autumnal colours, the sun shone and Seve was simply sensational. In a re-match with Frost he recorded 13 birdies, with no dropped shots, for the 29 holes needed to gain revenge over the South African in the most emphatic fashion (8 & 7). His morning round was, by his own admission, the best he had every played at Wentworth. It was sheer, undiluted brilliance.

Seve's vintage display clearly vindicated his inclusion and obviously stole the headlines but the three other first round matches were also not short on drama. In another low scoring encounter, Vijay Singh accounted for Swedish debutante Jesper Parnevik by 4 & 3, with a birdie blitz (9 in 14 holes) of his own. Colin Montgomerie, for the second year running, had an epic tussle with the plucky Yoshinori Mizumaki, before winning by 2 & 1. While Brad Faxon, after losing the previous two holes, made a six-footer on the final green to see off a disappointing Ian Woosnam by one hole.

Friday saw more beautiful weather and wonderful golf for the record crowds. With the exception of José-Maria Olazabal's comfortable 6 & 4 victory over Brad Faxon, all the quarter finals were close affairs, with two seeds (last year's finalists, Faldo and Pavin) amongst the casualties. In the battle of the Ryder Cup partners, Faldo (himself 10 under par for the match) recovered from being four down after

20 holes against Montgomerie, to be all square after 26, but Monty was a different proposition to the man he beat at the same stage three years earlier. When Faldo bunkered his drive at the last his fate was sealed. Corey Pavin lived to rue a nine foot victory putt which got away on the home green against Vijay Singh: the Fijian put paid to the holder with a winning par on the first extra hole. The match of the day, though, inevitably involved Seve. The crucial moment of his thrilling duel with US Open champion Ernie Els came in the afternoon, at the 15th, when Seve, just one down after winning the previous two holes, hooked wildly off the tee to lose the hole and, eventually, the match by 2 & 1. The fact that Seve had once again played marvellously, recording 13 birdies and a staggering seven 2s spoke volumes for the big South African. It was even more impressive considering it was his first ever match in the event. Victory over Seve, who had looked set for a record sixth title was a huge psychological boost for Els.

Perhaps understandably though, after the emotion of the Seve match, Els suffered a reaction on Saturday (when fog delayed proceedings by a couple of hours) and after 20 holes of his semi-final clash with Masters champion Olazabal, found himself four down. From that point onwards, the Spaniard, who had pipped him for the Volvo PGA title over the same course earlier in the year and who was hobbling with a hip injury, didn't win another hole as Ernie swept to a 2 & 1 victory. The other semi-final was a somewhat disappointing affair, but in a lively finish, after being all square with two to play, Montgomerie edged out Singh by one hole.

So the stage was set for a final between the two men who (along with Loren Roberts) had contested the US Open play-off, some four months earlier. Played in cooler conditions, it was captivating if not inspirational, and the verdict was the same as at Oakmont – victory for Els (by 4 & 2). Monty, had fought back well from being three down at the turn, to lunch all square and was only one down with four to play before Ernie applied the decisive screw.

The £160,000 first prize made a delightful present (a day before his 25th birthday) for the first debut winner since Greg Norman in 1980 and, after Ballesteros, the second youngest

Colin Montgomerie had no answer to the irresistible force

champion. From the moment he scored the event's first ever eagle at the 3rd on Friday, Ernie was setting records in the championship. With the inspiration of a certain five-time winning fellow countryman to draw on, one wonders how many more Matchplay titles will follow in the years ahead for this immensely talented player.

1994 TOYOTA WORLD MATCHPLAY CHAMPIONSHIP

October 13 - 16, Wentworth Club (West Course), Surrey

First Round
Vijay Singh (Fij) beat Jesper Parnevik (Swe) 4 & 3
Colin Montgomerie (Scot) beat Yoshinori Mizumaki (Jap) 2 & 1
Seve Ballesteros (Sp) beat David Frost (SA) 8 & 7
Brad Faxon (USA) beat Ian Woosnam (Wal) 1 hole
First round losers received £25,000 each

Second Round
Vijay Singh beat Corey Pavin (USA) at 37th
Colin Montgomerie beat Nick Faldo (Eng) 1 hole
Ernie Els (SA) beat Seve Ballesteros 2 & 1
José-Maria Olazabal (Sp) beat Brad Faxon 6 & 4
Second round losers received £35,000 each

Semi-Finals
Colin Montgomerie beat Vijay Singh 1 hole
Ernie Els beat José-Maria Olazabal 2 & 1

Play-off for Third & Fourth Places
José-Maria Olazabal beat Vijay Singh 2 & 1
Olazabal received £60,000; Singh £50,000

Final
Ernie Els beat Colin Montgomerie 4 & 2
Els received £160,000; Montgomerie £90,000

Ernie Els, South Africa's first World Matchplay champion since Gary Player

THE WORLD MATCHPLAY
ROLL · OF · HONOUR

YEAR	WINNER				
1964	Arnold Palmer	1974	Hale Irwin	1984	Seve Ballesteros
1965	Gary Player	1975	Hale Irwin	1985	Seve Ballesteros
1966	Gary Player	1976	David Graham	1986	Greg Norman
1967	Arnold Palmer	1977	Graham Marsh	1987	Ian Woosnam
1968	Gary Player	1978	Isao Aoki	1988	Sandy Lyle
1969	Bob Charles	1979	Bill Rogers	1989	Nick Faldo
1970	Jack Nicklaus	1980	Greg Norman	1990	Ian Woosnam
1971	Gary Player	1981	Seve Ballesteros	1991	Seve Ballesteros
1972	Tom Weiskopf	1982	Seve Ballesteros	1992	Nick Faldo
1973	Gary Player	1983	Greg Norman	1993	Corey Pavin
				1994	Ernie Els

1994 WPG EUROPEAN TOUR REVIEW

To Laura Davies, the Power; to Lotte Neumann, the Glory

According to the Ping Leaderboard, Laura Davies and Liselotte Neumann are the two best women golfers in the world. Both are marvellous ambassadors for the game, both are European and both won the US Open early in their careers. There ends any similarity.

If Laura is the Ferrari, Lotte is the Rolls Royce: force and fury, ease and elegance. There may be a huge contrast in their styles of play but there is a nice symmetry to their transatlantic achievements in 1994.

Laura Davies was the number one player in America – the first British golfer, male or female, ever to achieve that feat. She topped the LPGA Money List and won three US events including a Major championship. In Europe, Laura won twice and finished third on the WPG European Order of Merit.

Lotte Neumann did the reverse in '94. She headed the European Order of Merit – the first Swede, male or female, ever to do so. She claimed three victories, including Europe's Major title, the Weetabix British Open and came third on the LPGA Money List, winning twice on American soil.

Strangely, they rarely produced their very best golf in the same tournament, although if one wasn't creating headlines and sending shock waves around the world of women's

Europe's number one in 1994: Liselotte Neumann

golf, the other invariably was. Perhaps the one occasion when Laura and Lotte did produce the fireworks simultaneously occurred at Woburn, where they were paired together in the second round of the Weetabix British Open: Davies scored a 66 (seven under par) and Neumann a 67. Between them, they amassed an amazing 13 birdies and one eagle. It was Laura who scored the eagle when she struck her 6-iron approach at the 462 yards par five 18th to

(Above) Dottie Mochrie chased Lotte Neumann all the way at Woburn.
(Left) Leading moneywinner in America, England's Laura Davies captured the Irish and Scottish Open titles on the WPG European Tour

within nine inches of the flag. Lotte went on to win the championship with a four round total of 280 (12 under par).

No one had an answer to Neumann's consistency at Woburn – not even Dottie 'eyes of the tigress' Mochrie, who finished joint second with Annika Sorenstam – and no one had an answer to her brilliance at the Hennessy Cup in Cologne, where she retained her title with a sensational final round 65. Coming from four strokes back to overtake a high class field, Lotte described her closing score as, 'the best round of golf I have ever played'.

Neumann's third European victory took place in front of her home fans in the Trygg

Hansa Open. It was her most emphatic triumph as she finished four ahead of Australian runner up Corinne Dibnah and 10 ahead of Sorenstam who was third. Three wins from how many starts in Europe? Just four! (Bobby Jones would have been proud of such a strike rate). The one that 'got away' was the Scottish Open where she came joint sixth.

Laura Davies' two European wins in 1994 took place in successive weeks. At St Margaret's near Dublin she stormed to an eight stroke win in the Irish Open and then seven days later was victorious at the aforementioned Scottish Open at Dalmahoy. Her hatrick bid was thwarted by Neumann at Woburn.

Although Lotte and Laura clearly dominated (whenever they appeared) there were of course others who made an impression on the tour in 1994. The Swedes in general made a huge impression. Helen Alfredsson claimed the Tour's second biggest prize when she captured the inaugural Evian Masters tournament, staged beside the shores of Lake Geneva and, in front of record crowds, Catrin Nilsmark won the Ford Classic. Arguably more impressive, however, was the form of Annika Sorenstam,

Sweden's Solheim Cup stars: Annika Sorenstam (above) Helen Alfredsson (top right) and Catrin Nilsmark

who failed to win in Europe but in the five tournaments she entered never once finished outside the top five.

Among the year's most convincing victories was surely that achieved by Helen Wadsworth at the BMW Masters in Belgium. The Welsh golfer spread-eagled the field with opening rounds of 69-66 and thereafter was never seriously challenged. There were play-off wins for Corinne Dibnah and Julie Forbes and Belgium's 'fiery' Florence Descampe

rediscovered her form to win in Austria, but, like Wadsworth (and indeed French favourites Marie-Laure de Lorenzi and Sandrine Mendiburu), she lost it again in the crucial run up to the Solheim Cup and failed to be selected for the much awaited match at The Greenbrier (the Solheim Cup is reviewed ahead).

Finally, a mention for the rookies, who performed especially well in 1994. Leading the way were England's former Curtis Cup player, Joanne Morley, American Tracy Hanson and France's Patricia Meunier – who amazed everyone (including herself, apparently) by winning the English Open at Tytherington.

1994 WPG European Tour Summary

Weetabix
British
Open winner,
Lotte Neumann
had plenty to
smile about
in 1994

TOURNAMENT · WINNERS

Ford Classic	Catrin Nilsmark
Open Costa Azul	Sandrine Mendiburu
Evian Masters	Helen Alfredsson
OVB Damen Open	Florence Descampe
BMW European Masters	Helen Wadsworth
Hennessy Cup	Liselotte Neumann
Irish Holidays Open	Laura Davies
New Skoda Scottish Open	Laura Davies
Weetabix British Open	Liselotte Neumann
Trygg Hansa Open	Liselotte Neumann
Waterford Dairies English Open	Patricia Meunier
BMW Italian Open	Corinne Dibnah
Spanish Open	Marie-Laure de Lorenzi
Var French Open	Julie Forbes

August 11 - 14

WEETABIX WOMEN'S BRITISH OPEN

DUKE'S COURSE, WOBURN, BUCKINGHAMSHIRE

L Neumann	71	67	70	72	280	£52,500
D Mochrie	73	66	74	70	283	27,250
A Sorenstam	69	75	69	70	283	27,250
L Davies	74	66	73	71	284	14,625
C Dibnah	75	70	67	72	284	14,625
C Figg-Currier	69	74	68	74	285	10,750
H Alfredsson	71	76	71	68	286	9,250
T Hanson	74	73	66	74	287	8,000
S Strudwick	71	71	71	75	288	6,250
V Skinner	77	71	66	74	288	6,250
C Pierce	70	75	71	72	288	6,250
H Kobayashi	73	73	69	74	289	5,100
S Gautrey	69	74	72	75	290	4,800
T Abitbol	76	68	75	72	291	4,526
P Grice-Whittaker	77	72	72	70	291	4,526
M McGuire	71	73	78	69	291	4,526
S Gronberg Whitmore	71	69	74	78	292	4,100
L Wen-Lin	73	70	73	76	292	4,100
J Geddes	74	72	72	74	292	4,100
E Knuth	78	69	72	73	292	4,100

FORD · ORDER · OF · MERIT

1	Liselotte Neumann	£102,750
2	Helen Alfredsson	63,315
3	Laura Davies	59,384
4	Annika Sorenstam	58,360
5	Corinne Dibnah	57,040
6	Lora Fairclough	44,585
7	Tracy Hanson	44,205
8	Helen Wadsworth	41,979
9	Alison Nicholas	38,550
10	Karina Orum	34,613
11	Sarah Gautrey	34,547
12	Florence Descampe	31,862
13	Dale Reid	31,792
14	Marie-Laure de Lorenzi	31,593
15	Trish Johnson	31,309
16	Catrin Nilsmark	29,956
17	Joanne Morley	26,636
18	Sofia Gronberg Whitmore	26,543
19	Kristal Parker	24,613
20	Laura Navarro	22,870

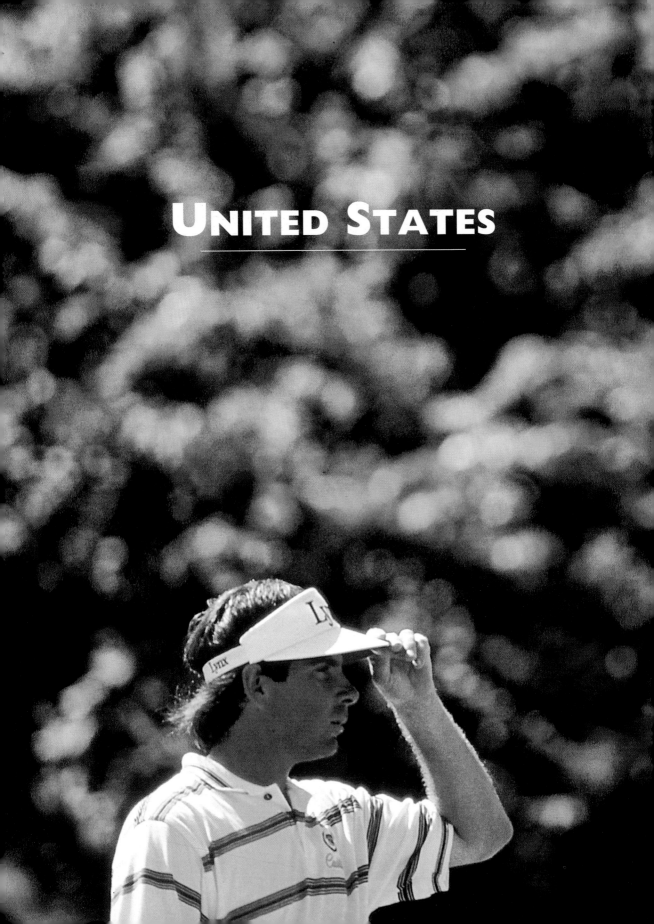

UNITED STATES

1994 US PGA TOUR REVIEW

by Joseph Mark Passov

Nick Price proved to the world in 1994 that he is better at hitting a golf ball and getting it into the hole than anybody else has been in a long, long time. That's not to say that several of his rivals didn't give spirited chase and produce the occasional masterly performance, notably Greg Norman and Spain's José-Maria Olazabal, merely that week in, week out Price was perceptibly superior.

All in all, the '94 season was a mixed bag. It produced an odd blend of young superstars ripening on cue and veteran heroes ageing nicely. As usual, the year saw several delightful surprises and, sadly, some crushing disappointments. And always, there was Price.

What exactly did Price do in 1994? Well, he won the money title for the second straight

In pursuit of greatness: Nick Price dominated the PGA Tour in 1994

year, failing by just $73 to reach a million and a half and he ran away with the Byron Nelson Award for most victories on tour with five, the largest number since Tom Watson bagged six in 1980. Only one other player could post three wins, the resurgent Mark McCumber, and only two men could boast a pair of victories: Olazabal, who wasn't even a PGA Tour member, and the unheralded Mike Springer.

By his own admission, Price wasn't as handy with the putter as he had been in '93, but his incomparable driving more than

the second time in three years, and also found time to defend successfully at the oldest regular US Tour event, the Western Open.

Do you want more evidence? Price extracted a final-round 64 to force a play-off in the Southwestern Bell Colonial, at storied Colonial Country Club in Fort Worth, Texas, a track known as 'Hogan's Alley', thanks to hometown boy Ben Hogan winning the event five times between 1946 and 1959. Seven shots in arrears when the rain-delayed final round began, Price capped a birdie assault by dropping an eight-

Greg Norman, on his way to an 'other-worldly' performance at The Players Championship in March

compensated. He led the tour's all-around driving statistical category, which combines the positions on the distance and accuracy charts. Always a long knocker, Price finished joint sixth in driving distance on 277.5 yards per average drive, and sent enough of those missiles down on the short grass to leave him with a seemingly endless succession of easy approach shots.

Oh, yes, Price also won the British Open in remarkable fashion, scored a runaway victory in the next major, the USPGA, staking that title for

foot birdie putt on the first sudden-death hole to defeat Scott Simpson. Price threw another 64 at the leaders in the final round at Memphis in a desperate bid to retain his title there, but came up one stroke shy of a play-off.

Two weeks after Memphis came Price's USPGA blitzkrieg, but even then he wasn't quite through. He still had one of golf's oldest national championships to claim, the Bell Canadian Open in September, which he won for the second time. Price edged ahead at the par five 16th hole, where he hit a 217 yard 2-

iron second shot that rolled to within 30 inches of the flag, leaving him a tap-in for an eagle three, which he duly converted.

'Probably the best 2-iron I've ever hit in my life,' said Price. He could have added that he'd just compiled an enviable career record six wins, including two major championships, plus a million dollars in prize money, all in the space of six months.

It took a little while for Price to make his mark in '94. Before he captured his first title, the Honda Classic in mid-March, where he

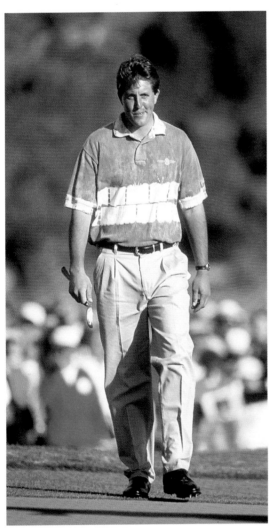

Phil Mickelson won the Mercedes Championship in January

edged Craig Parry by one stroke, countless interesting developments had already stirred the Tour.

Significant interest early on centred more on who was absent from tournaments than on who was present. Injuries and medical problems robbed the PGA Tour of three of its most appealing talents for much of the first half of the season. Paul Azinger, undergoing treatment for cancer, was absent until August. At the risk of sounding melodramatic, his comeback elicited an outpouring of emotion from fans, media and fellow competitors. Fred Couples suffered a back injury in March, which kept him sidelined until well into summer and Phil Mickelson broke his leg badly in a snowskiing accident in January, earning him a four month hiatus from tour activity.

The beleaguered west coast tournaments again suffered from depleted fields, devoid of superstars; it appears that many of the world's best are so active and making huge amounts of money during golf's 'silly season' of November and December, that they're choosing to bypass much of the west coast swing, preferring to practise and rest up for the Florida leg that begins in early March.

Before Couples and Mickelson were incapacitated, they duelled at the season's first stop, the Mercedes Championships at La Costa, near San Diego, in the event once known as the Tournament of Champions. Mickelson and Couples were tied after four rounds on 12 under par, 276. On the first play-off hole, Couples' drive took a hideous bounce, leaving him an impossible second. He cursed a blue streak on camera, made a quick double-bogey, and Mickelson secured the win.

One week later, Davis Love III scorched the Hawaiian Open's Waialae Country Club for a 12 under par 60 in the second round, but a pair of indifferent 71s left him a stroke back of Australian Brett Ogle on Sunday. Love's 60 was the sole individual highlight in a disappointing year that saw him sink from 12th to 33rd on the money list with barely a whimper.

1994 was a glorious year for the young lions, with Olazabal and Ernie Els, both in their twenties, grabbing major championships. Nonetheless, it was a truly remarkable year for the forty-somethings on tour, the men seemingly in the twilight of their careers, who were supposed to ease gracefully into the Senior Tour – not go out kicking and screaming and, more importantly, winning.

Unquestionably, the freakiest win of the year took place at Pebble Beach in early February, when Johnny Miller somehow conjured up long-lost magic and won the AT&T Pebble Beach Pro-Am. At 46, Miller became the first grandfather to win on tour since 1975, when 51 year old Art Wall won in Milwaukee. Miller is virtually retired from tournament golf; he designs golf courses now and is a full-time announcer on NBC-TV golf telecasts. So infrequent are Miller's tour appearances that Pebble Beach was his only scheduled event during the entire year.

Playing the best golf down the stretch at the AT & T was Tom Watson. For nostalgia fans, it was a dream come true watching Miller and Watson going down to the wire at Pebble Beach. For Watson fans, it was a dream turned nightmare, though, watching the man who was once golf's ablest holer of short putts miss a succession of them at crunch time, a trait that would plague him repeatedly on grand occasions throughout the year, most painfully at Augusta, Oakmont and Turnberry.

The Nissan Los Angeles Open at Riviera Country Club was next on the slate; how difficult it is to believe that Corey Pavin's win, by two shots from Fred Couples, would be his only one on tour in '94. Pavin was steady, compiling three runner-up finishes on his way

to an eighth-place finish on the money list. But Pavin carries with him a burden of expectation. Despite his ungainly swing, he is perhaps the PGA Tour's best and most imaginative ball-striker, and his putting prowess is rightly renowned. Both critics and supporters are waiting for Pavin to break through with more wins, and now that Olazabal has shed the 'best player never to have won a major' monkey from his back, it has fallen squarely on Pavin's.

Serving notice at the Bob Hope Chrysler Classic was 42 year old Fuzzy Zoeller, one of

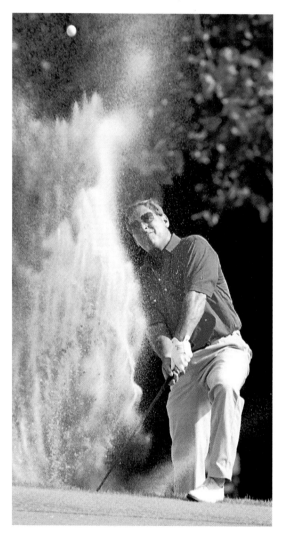

Fuzzy Zoeller enjoyed his best season for many-a-year

golf's most popular, enduring showmen. Zoeller had finished 39th on the 1993 money list, and some thought his best years were behind him. Instead, Zoeller collected five runner-up finishes in '93, the Bob Hope among them, won more than a million dollars, and finished fifth on the money list.

Zoeller did everything but win. He had the British Open in his grasp, until a bout of careless putting in the final round spoiled his

when he sliced a 4-iron at the par three 71st hole into the gallery then watched helplessly as the ball ricocheted off a spectator into water.

Nipping Zoeller, Price and Vijay Singh by a stroke at Bay Hill to win his first tour title was Loren Roberts, who would go on to elevate his status from journeyman to the new elite with his exceptional play throughout the year.

Ah, finally, we return to the curious case of Gregory John Norman. On February 10, 1995,

chances. He lost the season-ending Tour Championship at San Francisco's Olympic Club in a play-off. He rolled in birdies from everywhere at The Players Championship in March, shattering the tournament record in the process yet was still beaten by Greg Norman's other-worldly performance.

Most cruelly, he lost the Nestle Invitational at Arnold Palmer's Bay Hill Club in March

Norman will turn 40. He is still waging marvellous campaigns, and had an especially brilliant one on the US tour in 1994, finishing second on the money list with more than $1.3 million and claiming his third Vardon Trophy Award for best scoring average on tour, averaging an incredible 68.81 strokes per round.

Hush now, though, so you can hear the

whispers. Yes, Norman won only once on the US Tour all year. True, it was a mind-boggling performance, as he steamrolled the field at The Players Championship shooting 63-67-67-67 but... it was still his only win. It's hard to be too tough on Norman because for most of the year it seemed he was on the leaderboard every week, regardless of course or conditions. Norman has all the cash he needs; now he needs a bunch of victories to cement his status

via a self-imposed suspension.

Powerful Tom Lehman challenged Olazabal right to the end at The Masters, then grabbed Jack Nicklaus' Muirfield Village Golf Club by the back of the neck and shook it until it relinquished four 67s and the Memorial crown, in a performance that amazed even the Golden Bear.

1993 US Open champion Lee Janzen had a disappointing season, falling from seventh to

(Opposite page) Loren Roberts won the Nestle Invitational and lost a play-off for the US Open

Bamboozled and bamboozling: John Daly remains an enigma

as one of the game's all-time greats.

Several other tournaments and performances in 1994 merit comment. Hale Irwin stamped an exclamation point on an astounding year with a win at the MCI Heritage Classic at Harbour Town, 23 years after he first won the event. The 49 year old Irwin is fitter than most men half his age; he finished 19th on the earnings chart.

Popular anti-hero John Daly returned to the winner's circle at Atlanta in May, but by year's end, golf's biggest gallery draw (and surely its biggest enigma) had returned to the sidelines

35th on the money list, with just one top-three finish, a win at Westchester the week preceding the US Open. As Olazabal had done at New Orleans the week before The Masters, Ernie Els warmed up for Oakmont with a runner-up finish at Westchester.

Fred Couples returned from back ailments with a wildly popular win at Michigan's Buick Open in early August. He would then go on to win three successive events in November, including an unprecedented third successive triumph in the Heineken World Cup with partner Davis Love.

Olazabal chose not to play the US tour in 1995, but left his calling card at Akron's Firestone in late August, winning the World Series of Golf with rounds of 66-67-69-67. Ollie played just eight US events in 1994, yet won close to one million dollars.

We shouldn't neglect the year's most surprising comeback by 43 year old Mark McCumber. Never a superstar, but certainly a proven winner in his previous 16 years on tour, McCumber burst the dam open with three victories from July forward, culminating in a splendid performance against an elite field at the season-ending Tour Championship.

Finally, there's no sense dwelling on the shocking fall from form of Payne Stewart and Fulton Allem, both of whom skidded from the top 10 in '93 to something in the hundreds in '94. Each will surely embrace the rallying cry of the downtrodden, 'Wait 'till next year!'

Spanish raider, José-Maria Olazabal grabbed two of the Tour's greatest prizes: The Masters at Augusta and The World Series at Firestone

1994 PRESIDENTS CUP

Whether you take the view that the inaugural Presidents Cup was merely a meaningless celebration of golf and patriotism, or was instead an historic beginning of a revered event, one thing is undeniable: it is refreshingly entertaining to watch many of the world's top professionals competing at matchplay for pride and country, rather than for cash and Sony points.

Not everyone was willing to legitimise the newest team competition in golf. Tom Kite simply declined to play. Others, such as Tom Watson and Seve Ballesteros, criticised the derivative nature of the event, claiming it could detract from the now awe-inspiring Ryder Cup Matches, and to a lesser extent, draw attention away from other international team events.

Still, proponents felt the event filled a need for more significant matchplay competition with a nationalistic bent; plus, with the Presidents Cup, Nick Price and Greg Norman would get to join the party, which, after all, is the reason the event was created in the first place. It was as if a light bulb went on in the cartoon balloon above someone's head, blinking the notion, 'We can't get Price and Norman in the Ryder Cup. There must be some other way.'

That some other way was the Presidents Cup, contested over the lovely Robert Trent Jones Golf Club on Lake Manasses in Virginia, roughly 35 miles from Washington DC. The Club attracts plenty of Capitol Hill's top slicers, including President Clinton himself, but in mid September, it was host to some of golf's ruling elite.

If we may skip ahead to the end, after the smoke had cleared from three days of furious shooting, the US had triumphed by a 20-12 margin over an international team comprised of the world's top players outside of Europe. Reactions were positive.

'This is the most fun I've had in golf,' said Fred Couples, sounding like Tom Watson after a day at Royal Dornoch or Ballybunion. Much of Fred's mirth could be traced to his performance on the third and final day, where

Situated within striking distance of Capitol Hill, The Robert Trent Jones Golf Club at Lake Manasses was an appropriate venue for the first Presidents Cup

he provided the winning point for the United States with a one up victory over Nick Price.

'This event was great for golf,' said the always-gracious Price, exhausted after a gruelling, highly successful summer.

Couples spun his 9-iron approach shot on the 429 yards, par four 18th hole to within two feet of the cup, leaving him a tap-in, Presidents Cup-clinching birdie. How different from his wrenching, wayward 9-iron in a

opponents with a birdie barrage to take a 5-0 lead after the first day morning fourball matches.

'Birdies were flying around so fast I felt like I was in a duck blind,' said American hunter-golfer Jim Gallagher Jr, who teamed with John Huston to birdie five consecutive holes on the front nine on the way to a 4 and 2 win over the Australians Craig Parry and Robert Allenby.

Down by 7½ to 2½ after day one, Captain

Hampered by the enforced late withdrawal of Greg Norman, David Graham's International Team were no match for an inspired Hale Irwin-led US side

similar, albeit more stressful situation at The Belfry in the 1989 Ryder Cup. Couples today is simply a better, more mature player, and one who didn't lose a match during the competition.

Play began inauspiciously on Friday morning amidst a fog that delayed play for nearly two hours. Also missing in action was Greg Norman, one of the catalysts for creating the event, who was forced to withdraw from the competition due to an intestinal illness. Nevertheless, Norman disobeyed doctor's orders and flew to Virginia to be with his team on Sunday.

When play finally got underway, the Americans resembled tigers at a raw meat convention. They tore up the course and their

David Graham and the Internationals rallied strongly on day two, paced by Vijay Singh, who was involved in two victories. At one point Hale Irwin's US team had led by only 10-8, before a spurt of their own upped their lead to 12-8 heading into Sunday's singles.

Although many of Sunday's matches were close, the US pulled away, with Couples slamming the door. Said Irwin to his team after the victory, 'The feeling you have now is why you want to play in these things. Don't ever forget this feeling.'

Graham added, 'We were part of history. It doesn't matter who won. It matters that we played, we competed and we are all the better for it.' It was, all in all, a stellar debut for the Presidents Cup.

September 16-18

THE PRESIDENTS CUP

ROBERT TRENT JONES GC, LAKE MANASSES, WASHINGTON DC

Friday: Fourballs

C Pavin & J Maggert bt S Elkington & V Singh, 2 & 1

J Haas & S Hoch bt F Allem & D Frost, 6 & 5

D Love III & F Couples bt N Price & B Huges, I up

J Huston & J Gallagher bt C Parry & R Allenby, 4 & 2

T Lehman & P Mickelson bt F Nobilo & P Senior, 3 & 2

SESSION: US 5, INTERNATIONAL 0

Friday: Foursomes

H Irwin & L Roberts bt D Frost & F Allem, 3 & 1

J Haas & S Hoch bt C Parry & T Watanabe, 4 & 3

C Pavin & J Maggert lost to F Nobilo & R Allenby, 2 & 1

P Mickelson & T Lehman lost to S Elkington & V Singh, 2 & 1

D Love & J Gallagher halved with N Price & M McNulty

SESSION: US 2½, INTERNATIONAL 2½

Saturday: Fourballs

J Gallagher & J Huston lost to F Allem & M McNulty, 4 & 3

J Haas &S Hoch lost to T Watanabe & V Singh, 3 & 1

L Roberts & T Lehman lost to C Parry & B Hughes, 4 & 3

F Couples & D Love bt F Nobilo & R Allenby 2 up

P Mickelson & T Pavin halved with N Price & S Elkington

SESSION: US 1½, INTERNATIONAL 3½

Saturday: Foursomes

H Irwin & J Haas lost to D Frost & P Senior, 6 & 5

C Pavin & L Roberts bt C Parry & F Allem I up

J Maggert & J Huston lost to V Singh & S Elkington, 3 & 2

D Love & J Gallagher bt F Nobilo & R Allenby, 7 & 5

P Mickelson & T Lehman bt B Hughes & M McNulty, 3 & 2

SESSION: US 3, INTERNATIONAL 2

Sunday: Singles

J Haas bt M McNulty 4 & 3

J Gallagher bt T Watanabe 43

H Irwin bt R Allenby I up

J Huston lost to P Senior 3 & 2

J Maggert bt B Hughes 2 & I

F Couples bt N Price I up

P Mickelson halved with F Allem

T Lehman halved with V Singh

L Roberts halved with F Nobilo

D Love bt S Elkington I up

C Pavin lost to C Parry I up

SESSION: US 8, INTERNATIONAL 4

US 20, INTERNATIONAL 12

1994 US PGA TOUR RESULTS

January 6 - 9
MERCEDES CHAMPIONSHIP
LA COSTA CC, CARLSBAD CA

*Phil Mickelson	70	68	70	68	276	$180,000
Fred Couples	69	70	69	68	276	120,000
Tom Kite	73	68	69	68	278	80,000
Jay Haas	71	71	69	69	280	46,625
Davis Love III	71	69	72	68	280	46,625
Jeff Maggert	72	74	65	69	280	46,625
Scott Simpson	70	72	70	68	280	46,625
David Edwards	75	68	66	72	281	34,000
Howard Twitty	72	73	67	69	281	34,000
Greg Norman	70	73	69	70	282	31,000
Ben Crenshaw	71	70	69	73	283	28,250
Brett Ogle	69	72	71	71	283	28,250

January 13 - 16
UNITED AIRLINES HAWAIIAN OPEN
WAIALAE CC, HONOLULU, HI

Brett Ogle	66	66	69	68	269	$216,000
Davis Love III	68	60	71	61	270	129,600
John Huston	70	68	67	67	272	81,600
Corey Pavin	68	70	70	65	273	57,600
Jesper Parnevik	71	66	74	63	274	48,000
Craig Parry	66	70	72	67	275	41,700
Ted Tryba	69	71	68	67	275	41,700
David Ishii	70	67	69	70	276	31,200
Jeff Maggert	69	67	68	72	276	31,200

January 20 - 23
NORTHERN TELECOM OPEN
TUCSON NATIONAL, TUCSON, AZ

Andrew Magee	69	67	67	67	270	$198,000
Jay Don Blake	68	69	67	68	272	72,600
Loren Roberts	68	68	72	64	272	72,600
Vijay Singh	67	68	72	65	272	72,600
Steve Stricker	68	69	68	67	272	72,600
Olin Browne	70	70	66	67	273	39,600
Robert Gamez	66	71	71	66	274	35,475

January 27 - 30
PHOENIX OPEN
TPC OF SCOTTSDALE, PHOENIX, AZ

Bill Glasson	68	68	68	64	268	$216,000
Bob Estes	66	68	69	68	271	129,600
Blaine McCallister	67	69	69	67	272	62,400
Mike Springer	68	68	71	65	272	62,400
Rick Fehr	66	67	69	71	273	41,700
Tom Lehman	67	68	73	65	273	41,700
Fred Funk	69	69	70	66	274	32,400
Scott Hoch	72	66	67	69	274	32,400
Phil Mickelson	67	70	71	66	274	32,400
Steve Pate	68	69	69	68	274	32,400
Curtis Strange	71	70	69	64	274	32,400

*winner in play-off

Johnny Miller defeated Father Time (and Tom Watson) to win at Pebble Beach

February 3 - 6
AT & T PEBBLE BEACH NATIONAL PRO-AM
THREE COURSES AT PEBBLE BEACH, CA

Johnny Miller	68	72	67	74	281	$225,000
Jeff Maggert	68	72	72	70	282	82,500
Corey Pavin	69	71	71	71	282	82,500
Kirk Triplett	69	74	67	72	282	82,500
Tom Watson	69	67	72	74	282	82,500
Tom Lehman	69	68	73	73	283	45,000
Keith Clearwater	70	70	71	73	284	36,375
Jay Delsing	66	75	70	73	284	36,375
Dudley Hart	65	71	70	78	284	36,375
Blaine McCallister	68	71	72	73	284	36,375
Ted Tryba	70	70	70	74	284	36,375

February 10 - 13
NISSAN LOS ANGELES OPEN
RIVIERA CC, PACIFIC PALLISADES, CA

Corey Pavin	67	64	72	68	271	$180,000
Fred Couples	67	67	68	71	273	108,000
Chip Beck	66	71	72	68	277	68,000
Brad Faxon	70	71	68	69	278	48,000
David Frost	67	74	71	67	279	40,000
Peter Jacobsen	69	71	68	72	280	34,750
Tom Watson	69	71	71	69	280	34,750
Lennie Clements	68	74	68	71	281	28,000
Jay Delsing	67	72	69	73	281	28,000
Craig Stadler	68	69	71	73	281	28,000
Kirk Triplett	68	76	69	68	281	28,000

February 14 - 20
BOB HOPE CHRYSLER CLASSIC
FOUR COURSES AT PALM SPRINGS, CA

Scott Hoch	66	62	70	66	70	334	$198,000
Fuzzy Zoeller	70	67	66	68	66	337	82,133
Lennie Clements	67	69	61	72	68	337	82,133
Jim Gallagher Jnr	66	67	74	62	68	337	82,133
Payne Stewart	67	69	71	68	63	338	44,000
Guy Boros	66	67	68	69	69	339	36,850
Keith Clearwater	67	64	70	68	70	339	36,850
Paul Stankowski	67	66	69	68	69	339	36,850
Bob Estes	66	69	70	67	68	340	30,800

February 24 - 27
BUICK INVITATIONAL OF CALIFORNIA
TORREY PINES GC, SAN DIEGO, CA

Craig Stadler	67	67	68	66	268	$198,000
Steve Lowery	67	68	66	68	269	118,800
Phil Mickelson	68	69	69	64	270	74,800
Hal Sutton	68	68	67	69	272	52,800
Mark Carnevale	67	69	70	67	273	44,000
Bob Estes	70	67	67	70	274	36,850
Robin Freeman	68	67	71	68	274	36,850
Kirk Triplett	71	63	68	72	274	36,850
Mark Calcavecchia	69	72	69	65	275	28,600
Lennie Clements	66	69	68	72	275	28,600
Paul Goydos	68	70	70	67	275	28,600
Doug Martin	65	73	68	69	275	28,600

Californian Corey Pavin produced some spectacular golf to win the LA Open at The Riviera Country Club

March 3 - 6
DORAL-RYDER OPEN
DORAL CC, MIAMI FL

John Huston	70	68	70	66	274	$252,000
Billy Andrade	70	68	66	73	277	123,200
Brad Bryant	70	69	69	69	277	123,200
Jim Thorpe	68	72	68	71	279	57,866
D A Weibring	74	69	65	71	279	57,866
Lennie Clements	72	70	66	71	279	57,866
Bruce Lietzke	74	69	71	67	281	43,633
Greg Norman	71	74	69	67	281	43,633
Loren Roberts	73	70	69	69	281	43,633

March 10 - 13
HONDA CLASSIC
WESTERN HILLS CC, FT LAUDERDALE, FL

Nick Price	70	67	73	66	276	$198,000
Craig Parry	68	73	69	67	277	118,800
Brandel Chamblee	67	68	72	71	278	74,800
John Daly	69	70	73	68	280	43,312
Bernhard Langer	67	72	73	68	280	43,312
Davis Love III	68	71	70	71	280	43,312
Curtis Strange	71	67	72	70	280	43,312
David Edwards	70	72	69	71	282	34,100

March 17 - 20
THE NESTLE INVITATIONAL
BAY HILL, ORLANDO FL

Loren Roberts	70	70	68	67	275	$216,000
Nick Price	66	72	68	70	276	89,600
Vijay Singh	68	69	68	71	276	89,600
Fuzzy Zoeller	72	68	67	69	276	89,600
Larry Mize	68	69	71	69	277	48,000
Tom Lehman	72	67	68	71	278	41,700
Greg Norman	68	72	71	67	278	41,700
Tom Watson	69	70	67	73	279	37,200
Andrew Magee	70	67	69	74	280	34,800

*winner in play-off

March 24 - 27
THE PLAYERS CHAMPIONSHIP
TPC AT SAWGRASS, PONTE VEDRA, FL

Greg Norman	63	67	67	67	264	$450,000
Fuzzy Zoeller	66	67	68	67	268	270,000
Jeff Maggert	65	69	69	68	271	170,000
Hale Irwin	67	70	70	69	276	120,000
Nick Faldo	67	69	68	73	277	100,000
Brad Faxon	68	68	70	72	278	83,750
Davis Love III	68	66	70	74	278	83,750
Steve Lowery	68	74	69	67	278	83,750
Gary Hallberg	68	69	69	73	279	65,000

March 31 - April 3
FREEPORT-MCMORAN CLASSIC
ENGLISH TURN G & CC, NEW ORLEANS, LA

Ben Crenshaw	69	68	68	68	273	$216,000
José-Maria Olazabal	63	74	70	69	276	129,600
Sam Torrance	67	71	67	73	278	81,600
Dennis Paulson	74	62	75	68	279	49,600
Kenny Perry	69	72	68	70	279	49,600
Mike Springer	73	69	69	68	279	49,600
Steve Brodie	71	67	72	71	281	36,150
Bobby Clampett	70	68	72	71	281	36,150
Chris Dimarco	76	70	66	69	281	36,150
Dick Mast	71	69	74	67	281	36,150

April 7 - 10
THE MASTERS TOURNAMENT
AUGUSTA NATIONAL GC, AUGUSTA, GA

(See page 33)

April 14 - 17
MCI HERITAGE GOLF CLASSIC
HARBOUR TOWN GL, HILTON HEAD, SC

Hale Irwin	68	65	65	68	266	$225,000
Greg Norman	67	66	67	68	268	135,000
Loren Roberts	69	70	68	62	269	85,000
David Edwards	70	71	65	64	270	51,666
David Frost	70	61	72	67	270	51,666
Nolan Henke	69	69	66	66	270	51,666
Russ Cochran	67	67	66	71	271	40,312

Bob Estes	65	70	68	68	271	40,312
Larry Mize	67	65	75	65	272	35,000
Jesper Parnevik	68	68	69	67	272	35,000
Jim McGovern	67	65	73	70	275	31,250
Fred Funk	65	70	71	70	276	27,500
Peter Jacobsen	68	68	71	69	276	27,500

April 21 - 24
K-Mart Greater Greensboro Open
FOREST OAKS CC, GREENSBORO, NC

Mike Springer	64	69	70	72	275	$270,000
Brad Bryant	68	71	68	71	278	112,000
Ed Humenik	72	65	73	68	278	112,000
Hale Irwin	65	73	71	69	278	112,000
Bob Lohr	69	71	69	70	279	60,000
Donnie Hammond	70	71	69	70	280	52,125
John Morse	72	68	67	73	280	52,125
David Edwards	71	74	68	68	281	42,000
Joel Edwards	69	69	73	70	281	42,000
Dudley Hart	75	69	67	70	281	42,000
Mike Smith	69	73	69	70	281	42,000

April 28 - May 1
Shell Houston Open
TPC AT THE WOODLANDS, TX

Mike Heinen	67	68	69	68	272	$234,000
Jeff Maggert	70	66	68	71	275	97,066
Hal Sutton	68	70	68	69	275	97,066
Tom Kite	68	65	71	71	275	97,066
Bob Gilder	66	76	69	67	278	49,400
Vijay Singh	72	67	69	70	278	49,400

John Daly	68	74	70	67	279	40,516
Gil Morgan	70	71	72	66	279	40,615
Peter Jacobsen	68	73	69	69	279	40,516

May 5 - 8
BellSouth Classic
ATLANTA CC, MARIETTA, GA

John Daly	69	64	69	72	274	$216,000
Nolan Henke	70	67	69	69	275	105,600
Brian Henninger	68	67	69	71	275	105,600
Bob Estes	71	69	68	68	276	52,800
David Peoples	73	65	68	70	276	52,800
Lennie Clements	68	69	72	68	277	38,850
Russ Cochran	69	69	69	70	277	38,850
Tom Kite	66	72	68	71	277	38,850
Blaine McCallister	69	68	69	71	277	38,850

May 13 - 16
GTE Byron Nelson Classic
TPC AT LAS COLINAS, IRVING, TX

*Neal Lancaster	67	65	132	$216,000
Tom Byrum	68	64	132	72,000
Mark Carnevale	65	67	132	72,000
David Edwards	67	65	132	72,000
Yoshinori Mizumaki	66	66	132	72,000
David Ogrin	64	68	132	72,000
Brad Bryant	66	67	133	40,200

May 19 - 22
Memorial Tournament
MUIRFIELD VILLAGE GC, DUBLIN, OH

Tom Lehman	67	67	67	67	268	$270,000
Greg Norman	70	69	70	64	273	162,000
John Cook	67	69	69	71	276	102,000
Donnie Hammond	69	69	70	69	277	72,000
David Edwards	69	67	72	70	278	60,000
Robert Gamez	77	69	66	67	279	54,000
Mark Brooks	64	75	70	71	280	48,375
Ben Crenshaw	72	66	74	68	280	48,375
Brad Faxon	72	68	72	69	281	42,000
Jeff Maggert	71	74	66	70	281	42,000

Jack Nicklaus and Tom Lehman at Muirfield Village

May 26 - 29
SOUTHWESTERN BELL COLONIAL
COLONIAL CC, FORT WORTH, TX

*Nick Price	65	70	67	64	266	$252,000
Scott Simpson	66	65	64	71	266	151,200
Hale Irwin	64	70	68	65	267	95,200
Peter Jordan	68	70	66	66	270	67,200
Brad Faxon	70	66	67	68	271	51,100
Gary Hallberg	67	67	65	72	271	51,100
Tom Lehman	66	66	69	70	271	51,100
Phil Mickelson	68	68	71	65	272	43,400
John Cook	66	71	67	70	274	37,800
Mark McCumber	68	69	67	70	274	37,800
Corey Pavin	68	67	69	70	274	37,800

June 2 - 5
KEMPER OPEN
TPC AT AVENEL, POTOMAC, MD

Mark Brooks	65	68	69	69	271	$234,000
Bobby Wadkins	68	67	65	74	274	114,400
D A Weibring	70	68	68	68	274	114,400
Lee Janzen	70	71	68	66	275	57,200
Phil Mickelson	70	69	67	69	275	57,200
Joel Edwards	71	70	68	69	278	46,800
Craig Parry	69	71	69	70	279	40,516
Kenny Perry	72	72	68	67	279	40,516
Mark Lye	70	70	69	70	279	40,516

June 9 - 12
BUICK CLASSIC
WESTCHESTER CC, RYE, NY

Lee Janzen	69	69	64	66	268	$216,000
Ernie Els	68	66	69	68	271	129,600
Brad Faxon	70	68	70	66	274	69,600
Jay Haas	68	70	69	67	274	69,600
Billy Andrade	70	71	66	69	276	43,800
Bob Burns	71	67	70	68	276	43,800
Steve Pate	66	72	69	69	276	43,800
Mark Brooks	71	70	66	70	277	32,400
Robin Freeman	69	69	69	70	277	32,400
Hale Irwin	70	72	65	70	277	32,400
Jeff Maggert	72	72	64	69	277	32,400

June 17 - 20
US OPEN
OAKMONT CC, OAKMONT, PA

(See page 45)

June 23 - 26
CANON GREATER HARTFORD OPEN
TPC AT RIVER HIGHLANDS, CROMWELL, CT

David Frost	65	68	66	69	268	$216,000
Greg Norman	69	65	66	69	269	129,600
Corey Pavin	65	73	66	67	271	57,600
Dave Stockton Jnr	66	66	67	72	271	57,600
Steve Stricker	70	67	67	67	271	57,600
Dave Barr	68	70	68	65	271	57,600
Kirk Triplett	71	66	69	67	273	38,700
Wayne Levi	68	66	71	68	273	38,700

June 30 - July 3
MOTOROLA WESTERN OPEN
COG HILL CC, LEMONT, IL

Nick Price	67	67	72	71	277	$216,000
Greg Kraft	67	70	68	73	278	129,600
Mark Calcavecchia	67	70	72	70	279	62,400
Bill Glasson	66	70	72	71	279	62,400
Scott Hoch	67	69	73	70	270	62,400
Kelly Gibson	69	72	72	67	280	41,700
Jeff Sluman	68	69	69	74	280	41,700

July 6 - 10
ANHEUSER-BUSCH GOLF CLASSIC
KINGSMILL GC, WILLIAMSBURG, VA

Mark McCumber	67	69	65	66	267	$198,000
Glen Day	64	68	72	66	270	118,800
Justin Leonard	67	69	67	69	272	74,800
Michael Bradley	68	69	69	67	273	45,466
John Wilson	64	70	72	67	273	45,466
Scott Verplank	71	69	66	67	273	45,466
Jay Haas	69	73	65	67	274	34,283
Tommy Armour III	69	71	67	67	274	34,283

*winner in play-off

July 11 - 17
DEPOSIT GUARANTY GOLF CLASSIC
HATTIESBURG CC, HATTIESBURG, MS

*Brian Henninger	67	68	135	$126,000
Mike Sullivan	66	69	135	75,600
Tommy Armour III	71	65	136	31,570
Guy Boros	69	67	136	31,570
Chris Dimarco	70	66	136	31,570
Scott Hoch	69	67	136	31,570
Dave Stockton Jnr	69	67	136	31,570

July 21 - 24
NEW ENGLAND CLASSIC
PLEASANT VALLEY CC, SUTTON, MA

Kenny Perry	67	66	70	65	268	$180,000
David Feherty	65	69	68	67	269	108,000
Ed Fiori	66	66	70	70	272	68,000
Chris Dimarco	67	68	70	68	273	48,000
Steve Gotsche	68	70	69	67	274	40,000
Billy Downes	71	68	69	67	275	33,500
Fred Funk	68	66	75	66	275	33,500
Justin Leonard	69	68	70	68	275	33,500

July 27 - 31
FEDERAL EXPRESS ST JUDE CLASSIC
TPC AT SOUTHWIND, MEMPHIS, TN

*Dicky Pride	66	67	67	67	267	$225,000
Gene Sauers	67	66	68	66	267	110,000
Hal Sutton	67	68	68	64	267	110,000
Nick Price	72	66	66	64	268	60,000
Dave Barr	66	69	67	67	269	45,625
Russ Cochran	67	68	65	69	269	45,625
Wayne Grady	70	66	67	66	269	45,625
Paul Stankowski	68	67	69	66	270	37,500
Fuzzy Zoeller	66	65	70	69	270	37,500

August 4 - 7
BUICK OPEN
WARWICK HILLS G & CC, GRAND BLANC, MI

Fred Couples	72	65	65	68	270	$198,000
Corey Pavin	66	65	70	71	272	118,800
Greg Kraft	71	72	67	66	276	57,200

Steve Pate	71	67	69	69	276	57,200
Curtis Strange	71	70	67	68	276	57,200
Keith Clearwater	71	67	69	70	277	38,225
Ben Crenshaw	72	68	69	68	277	38,225
Fred Funk	65	70	71	72	278	31,900
Tom Lehman	71	67	70	70	278	31,900
Duffy Waldorf	69	67	74	68	278	31,900

August 11 - 14
PGA CHAMPIONSHIP
SOUTHERN HILLS CC, TULSA, OKLA

(See page 71)

August 18 - 21
SPRINT INTERNATIONAL
CASTLE PINES GC, CASTLE ROCK, CO

*Steve Lowery	35	$252,000
Rick Fehr	35	151,200
Duffy Waldorf	34	95,200
Ernie Els	33	67,200
Tom Kite	32	56,000
John Adams	31	48,650
Chris Dimarco	31	48,650
Mark Calcavecchia	30	42,000
Dave Stockton Jnr	30	42,000
Phil Mickelson	29	36,400
Mike Reid	29	36,400

August 25 -28
NEC WORLD SERIES OF GOLF
FIRESTONE CC, AKRON, OH

José-Maria Olazabal	66	67	69	67	269	$360,000
Scott Hoch	71	64	65	70	270	216,000
Brad Faxon	69	68	65	69	271	116,000
Steve Lowery	67	66	66	72	271	116,000
John Huston	73	64	64	71	272	76,000
Mark McNulty	69	68	65	70	272	76,000
Mike Heinen	71	67	65	70	273	67,000
Fred Couples	69	70	65	70	274	60,000
Greg Norman	67	67	68	72	274	60,000
Hale Irwin	70	65	71	70	276	52,000
Nick Price	68	66	69	73	276	52,000

September 1 - 4
GREATER MILWAUKEE OPEN
TACKAWAY CC, FRANKLIN, WI

Mike Springer	69	67	65	67	268	$180,000
Loren Roberts	70	63	68	68	269	108,000
Mark Calcavecchia	67	68	64	71	270	48,000
Bob Estes	67	66	65	72	270	48,000
Tom Purtzer	70	69	67	64	270	48,000
Joey Sindelar	67	68	66	69	270	48,000
Dave Barr	69	64	70	68	271	32,250
Marco Dawson	68	66	69	68	271	32,250

September 8 - 11
BELL CANADIAN OPEN
GLEN ABBEY GC, OAKVILLE, ONTARIO

Nick Price	67	72	68	68	275	$234,000
Mark Calcavecchia	67	71	71	67	276	140,400
Tom Lehman	69	69	70	69	277	88,400
Jay Don Blake	74	63	73	68	278	57,200
Mark McCumber	74	65	67	72	278	57,200
Fulton Allem	69	69	71	70	279	43,550
Brian Kamm	71	71	69	68	279	43,550
Steve Stricker	69	70	69	71	279	43,550
Mark O'Meara	66	72	72	70	280	37,700
Bob Estes	72	73	68	68	281	32,500
Payne Stewart	68	72	72	69	281	32,500

September 15 - 18
B C OPEN
EN-JOIE GC, ENDICOTT, NY

Mike Sullivan	65	67	68	66	266	$162,000
Jeff Sluman	63	68	67	72	270	97,200
Brian Claar	68	68	65	71	272	52,200
Mike Hulbert	67	67	68	70	272	52,200
Russell Beiersdorf	69	66	68	70	273	34,200
Curt Byrum	67	69	66	71	273	34,200
Bill Glasson	70	65	68	71	274	28,050
Paul Goydos	68	68	67	71	274	28,050
Blaine McCallister	67	70	65	72	274	28,050

September 22 - 25
HARDEE'S GOLF CLASSIC
OAKWOOD, COAL VALLEY, IL

Mark McCumber	66	67	65	67	265	$180,000
Kenny Perry	67	66	65	68	266	108,000
Mike Donald	70	66	64	67	267	58,000
David Frost	68	67	67	65	267	58,000
Russ Cochran	67	66	70	65	268	40,000
Curt Byrum	69	65	65	70	269	32,375
John Huston	71	66	67	65	269	32,375
Tom Lehman	71	67	65	66	269	32,375
Robert Wrenn	63	70	67	69	269	32,375

During an incredible ten week spell Nick Price won the British Open at Turnberry, the PGA Championship at Southern Hills and the Canadian Open at Glen Abbey

September 29 - October 2
BUICK SOUTHERN OPEN
CALLAWAY GDNS, PINE MOUNTAINS, GA

Steve Elkington	66	66	68	200	$144,000
Steve Rintoul	70	65	70	205	86,400
Brad Bryant	70	68	69	207	54,400
Buddy Gardner	71	69	68	208	33,066
Steve Pate	69	71	68	208	33,066
Gene Sauers	72	67	69	208	33,066

October 6 - 9
WALT DISNEY WORLD/OLDSMOBILE CLASSIC
THREE COURSES AT LAKE BUENA VISTA, FL

Rick Fehr	63	70	68	68	269	$198,000
Craig Stadler	68	66	67	70	271	96,800
Fuzzy Zoeller	66	70	69	66	271	96,800
Trevor Dodds	68	66	70	68	272	48,400
Steve Stricker	72	67	66	67	272	48,400
Robert Gamez	68	69	68	68	273	39,600
Glen Day	65	68	72	69	274	33,137
Donnie Hammond	68	72	67	67	274	33,137

October 13 - 16
TEXAS OPEN
OAK HILLS CC, SAN ANTONIO, TX

Bob Estes	62	65	68	70	265	$180,000
Gil Morgan	66	68	65	67	266	108,000
Don Pooley	69	65	65	68	267	68,000
Bruce Lietzke	68	69	64	69	270	48,000
Mark McNulty	70	65	67	69	271	36,500
Craig Stadler	68	66	69	68	271	36,500
John Wilson	66	68	67	70	271	36,500
Ben Crenshaw	70	69	68	65	272	25,000

October 17 - 23
LAS VEGAS INVITATIONAL
THREE COURSES AT LAS VEGAS, NV

Bruce Lietzke	66	67	68	66	65	332	$270,000
Robert Gamez	66	70	64	69	64	333	162,000
Billy Andrade	66	68	67	67	67	335	87,000
Phil Mickelson	70	66	66	70	63	335	87,000
Jim Furyk	61	64	69	66	70	336	54,750
Bill Glasson	67	68	70	65	66	336	54,750
Paul Stankowski	70	66	66	69	65	336	54,750
Guy Boros	70	63	67	68	69	337	42,000
Scott Hoch	66	63	70	70	68	337	42,000
Sean Murphy	64	69	67	69	68	337	42,000
Kirk Triplett	69	65	65	68	70	337	42,000

October 27 - 30
TOUR CHAMPIONSHIP
OLYMPIC CLUB, SAN FRANCISCO, CA

*Mark McCumber	66	71	69	68	274	$540,000
Fuzzy Zoeller	71	69	66	68	274	324,000
Brad Bryant	72	68	67	68	275	207,000
David Frost	66	69	75	66	276	132,000
Bill Glasson	66	68	71	71	276	132,000
Jay Haas	69	71	71	66	277	108,000
Jeff Maggert	72	66	70	70	278	102,000
Steve Lowery	66	69	72	72	279	93,000
Loren Roberts	71	70	68	70	279	93,000
John Huston	74	68	66	72	280	81,000
Bruce Lietzke	69	71	71	69	280	81,000
Corey Pavin	69	69	70	72	280	81,000
Ben Crenshaw	72	70	69	70	281	71,400
Greg Norman	69	75	66	71	281	71,400

*winner in play-off

Mark McCumber captured the Tour Championship in San Francisco after a play-off with Fuzzy Zoeller

1994 US PGA TOUR

TOURNAMENT · WINNERS

January

MERCEDES CHAMPIONSHIPS	Phil Mickelson	(US)
UNITED AIRLINES HAWAIIAN OPEN	Brett Ogle	(aUS)
NORTHERN TELECOM OPEN	Andrew Magee	(US)
PHOENIX OPEN	Bill Glasson	(US)

February

AT&T PEBBLE BEACH NATIONAL PRO-AM	Johnny Miller	(US)
NISSAN LOS ANGELES OPEN	Corey Pavin	(US)
BOB HOPE CHRYSLER CLASSIC	Scott Hoch	(US)
BUICK INVITATIONAL OF CALIFORNIA	Craig Stadler	(US)

March

DORAL-RYDER OPEN	John Huston	(US)
HONDA CLASSIC	Nick Price	(Zim)
THE NESTLE INVITATIONAL	Loren Roberts	(US)
THE PLAYERS CHAMPIONSHIP	Greg Norman	(Aus)
FREEPORT-MCMORAN CLASSIC	Ben Crenshaw	(US)

April

THE MASTERS	José-Maria Olazabal	(Sp)
MCI HERITAGE CLASSIC	Hale Irwin	(US)
KMART GREATER GREENSBORO OPEN	Mike Springer	(US)
SHELL HOUSTON OPEN	Mike Heinen	(US)

May

BELLSOUTH CLASSIC	John Daly	(US)
GTE BYRON NELSON CLASSIC	Neal Lancaster	(US)
MEMORIAL TOURNAMENT	Tom Lehman	(US)
SOUTHWESTERN BELL COLONIAL	Nick Price	(Zim)

June

KEMPER OPEN	Mark Brooks	(US)
BUICK CLASSIC	Lee Janzen	(US)
US OPEN	Ernie Els	(SA)
CANON GREATER HARTFORD OPEN	David Frost	(SA)
MOTOROLA WESTERN OPEN	Nick Price	(Zim)

July

ANHEUSER-BUSCH GOLF CLASSIC	Mark McCumber	(US)
DEPOSIT GUARANTY GOLF CLASSIC	Brian Henninger	(US)
THE NEW ENGLAND CLASSIC	Kenny Perry	(US)
FEDERAL EXPRESS ST JUDE CLASSIC	Dicky Pride	(US)

August

BUICK OPEN	Fred Couples	(US)
PGA CHAMPIONSHIP	Nick Price	(Zim)
THE INTERNATIONAL	Steve Lowery	(US)
NEC WORLD SERIES OF GOLF	José-Maria Olazabal	(Sp)

September

GREATER MILWAUKEE OPEN	Mike Springer	(US)
BELL CANADIAN OPEN	Nick Price	(Zim)
BC OPEN	Mike Sullivan	(US)
PRESIDENTS CUP	USA 20, International Team 12	
HARDEE'S CLASSIC	Mark McCumber	(US)
BUICK SOUTHERN OPEN	Steve Elkington	(Aus)

October

WALT DISNEY WORLD/ OLDSMOBILE CLASSIC	Rick Fehr	(US)
TEXAS OPEN	Bob Estes	(US)
LAS VEGAS INVITATIONAL	Bruce Lietzke	(US)
TOUR CHAMPIONSHIP	Mark McCumber	(US)

November

LINCOLN-MERCURY KAPALUA INTERNATIONAL	Fred Couples	(US)

1994
US PGA TOUR

LEADING MONEY WINNERS

Nick Price and Greg Norman:
great friends and great rivals

#	Name	Winnings	#	Name	Winnings	#	Name	Winnings
1	Nick Price	$1,499,927						
2	Greg Norman	1,330,307						
3	Mark McCumber	1,208,209						
4	Tom Lehman	1,031,144				66	Brett Ogle	284,495
5	Fuzzy Zoeller	1,016,804				67	Fred Funk	281,905
6	Loren Roberts	1,015,671				68	Chip Beck	281,131
7	José-Maria Olazabal	969,900				69	Greg Kraft	279,901
8	Corey Pavin	906,305				70	Nolan Henke	278,419
9	Jeff Maggert	814,475				71	Duffy Waldorf	274,971
10	Hale Irwin	814,436				72	D A Weibring	255,757
11	Scott Hoch	804,559				73	Gene Sauers	250,654
12	Steve Lowery	794,048	39	Lennie Clements	416,880	74	Ted Tryba	246,481
13	Mike Springer	770,717	40	Mike Heinen	390,963	75	Paul Goydos	241,107
14	Bob Estes	765,360	41	Curtis Strange	390,881	76	Guy Boros	240,775
15	Phil Mickelson	748,316	42	Larry Mize	386,029	77	Russ Cochran	239,827
16	John Huston	731,499	43	Tom Watson	380,378	78	Jim Furyk	236,603
17	Bill Glasson	689,110	44	Robert Gamez	380,353	79	Jim McGovern	227,764
18	Brad Bryant	687,803	45	Glen Day	357,236	80	Bob Lohr	225,048
19	Ernie Els	684,440	46	Craig Parry	354,602	81	Johnny Miller	225,000
20	David Frost	671,683	47	Blaine McCallister	351,554	82	Gary Hallberg	224,965
21	Ben Crenshaw	659,252	48	Billy Andrade	342,208	83	Nick Faldo	221,146
22	Tom Kite	658,689	49	John Daly	340,034	84	Mike Hulbert	221,007
23	Fred Couples	625,654	50	Steve Stricker	334,409	85	Chris Dimarco	216,839
24	Brad Faxon	612,847	51	Jim Gallagher Jr	325,976	86	Mark O'Meara	214,070
25	Jay Haas	593,386	52	Vijay Singh	325,959	87	Colin Montgomerie	213,828
26	Kenny Perry	585,941	53	Dave Barr	314,885	88	Peter Jacobsen	211,762
27	Rick Fehr	573,963	54	Gil Morgan	309,690	89	Bobby Wadkins	208,358
28	Bruce Lietzke	564,926	55	Jay Don Blake	309,351	90	Keith Clearwater	203,549
29	Hal Sutton	540,162	56	Scott Simpson	307,884	91	Wayne Levi	200,476
30	Mark Calcavecchia	533,201	57	Dicky Pride	305,769	92	David Ogrin	199,199
31	Mark Brooks	523,285	58	Neal Lancaster	305,038	93	Mark Carnevale	192,653
32	Craig Stadler	474,831	59	Jeff Sluman	301,178	94	Tom Purtzer	187,307
33	Davis Love III	474,219	60	Mike Sullivan	298,586	95	Jim Thorpe	185,714
34	David Edwards	458,845	61	Donnie Hammond	295,436	96	Dave Stockton Jr	185,209
35	Lee Janzen	442,588	62	Steve Elkington	294,943	97	Scott Verplank	183,015
36	Andrew Magee	431,041	63	Brian Henninger	294,075	98	Brian Kamm	181,884
37	John Cook	429,725	64	Steve Pate	291,651	99	Mike Standly	179,850
38	Kirk Triplett	422,171	65	Clark Dennis	289,065	100	David Feherty	178,501

1994 LPGA TOUR REVIEW

by Joseph Mark Passov

It was a season of surprises and a year of puzzles. One surprise – that perhaps should come as no surprise – was the smashing return to form of three of the game's established superstars, England's Laura Davies, America's Beth Daniel and Sweden's Liselotte Neumann, who finished 1-2-3 on the money list. Laura dominated the first half of the season, Lotte the second half, and Beth was superb throughout. This followed an off-year (by their standards) on the LPGA Tour in '93, when Davies finished 29th on the money list, Daniel 49th, and Neumann a dismal 57th.

More surprising were the fatal plunges suffered by several golfers, notably injury-prone Brandie Burton who dropped from third to 31st in earnings, Rosie Jones who fell from 11th to 42nd and especially 1992 Solheim Cup competitor Danielle Ammaccapane, who plummeted from third in '92 to 28th in '93, then vanished entirely from the top 75 in '94.

In the puzzling category were Dottie Mochrie, Meg Mallon and Michelle McGann, all of whom had excellent years by any objective standard, but of whom so much more was expected. Of the three, Mochrie had the best year, with one victory and fourth place on the money list, but she, like the others, simply couldn't hole those timely putts that would have propelled her to big wins.

In a category by herself was the always entertaining, usually exasperating Helen

Alfredsson. The Swedish golfer reminds some of a frazzled concert pianist, harnessing incredible talent in her hands and fingers, but capable of exploding at any moment. Alfredsson was true to form in '94.

Knocking on the door, right where we left them last year, were Amy Alcott and Betsy King. Both remain stuck at 29 tour wins, one short of the magical number for inclusion to the LPGA Hall of Fame. Alcott produced a brief

Although four-time winner Beth Daniel (opposite page) scooped most of the year-end honours, Laura Davies (right) was the LPGA Tour's Leading Moneywinner

flurry of good play in mid-summer and actually improved on her 1993 money position but she was unable to break through.

King's frustrations had to be particularly acute, as she lost leads in several events on the final day. When it came to the tour's concluding tournament, the Toray Japan Queens Cup, where she had notched her 29th win a year earlier, she again failed to convert despite a final round lead, and eventually lost in a play-off to Woo-Soon Ko.

Top newcomer of 1994 goes to Sweden's Annika Sorenstam, who posted a trio of top ten finishes, including joint second at the Weetabix Women's British Open on her way to a 39th place finish on the money list.

Only four women on the LPGA Tour won

more than one event in '94, Davies, Daniel, Neumann and Donna Andrews, the Pinehurst, NC resident with the elegant swing. Davies and Andrews met head-on in late March at the Nabisco Dinah Shore and produced the year's most dramatic finish.

The two players waged the equivalent of match play from the 12th hole forward in Sunday's final round. Andrews, who had captured the Ping/Welch's Championship at Tucson, two weeks earlier, fell one stroke behind with a bogey to Davies' par at the penultimate hole, thanks in part to a 'fat' 5-iron approach.

Davies, who dominated the field a week earlier in winning at Phoenix, chose a 4-iron for her tee shot at the 526 yards, par five 72nd hole. This she pushed to the right into the light rough, then followed with a 2-iron which found more rough. Andrews was first to play her approach, after successfully finding the fairway twice with two 3-woods. From 135 yards out, she uncorked a splendid knock-down 6-iron into the wind, planting the ball six feet from the hole.

Davies, meanwhile, selected an 8-iron for her third, but hit it heavy. Her ball finished at the far left of the green, with the hole cut far right. Her 60 foot birdie putt attempt would have to go uphill, then downhill. It tried to do what it was supposed to do, but came up eight feet short. Davies hadn't lost her turn; she putted again – and missed. Andrews quickly stepped up and coaxed her putt in for the birdie and the victory.

'As I looked at the putt, I remembered I sank a similar putt for a par on the last hole

Asked in the interview room how the victory felt, the barefoot Andrews responded, 'It's awesome. I don't think it will sink in for a long time.' In a nautical conclusion to the year's first major championship, Andrews sank a putt, took a swim, then tried to let the feeling sink in.

Another magnificent confrontation took place in mid-July, at New York's JAL Big Apple Classic, when Davies roared from behind with a

Patty Sheehan (right) took advantage of a dramatic weekend collapse by Helen Alfredsson (below) to win her second US Women's Open at Indianwood

yesterday,' Andrews said. 'I told my husband (her caddie) I wouldn't leave it short. I learned my lesson as a rookie.'

Andrews celebrated her triumph in what is now standard fashion at the Dinah Shore, by leaping into the lake next to the 18th green.

final round five under par 66 to tie Beth Daniel for the title. Daniel had finished with a par 71, making the play-off by holing a closing five-foot birdie putt on the 475-yards par five.

Minutes later, Daniel snared the title at the 18th, the first play-off hole, by dropping a six-foot birdie putt, then watching as Davies missed her try from four feet.

'I'm not very good at play-offs,' Davies said. 'This is the seventh I've lost. It came down to that one putt. In a situation like that, the first one who holes is going to be the winner.'

Nonetheless, Davies had enough victories (three) and enough top-three finishes (eight), to take the money crown with $687,201. Daniel was second with $659,426, but won the Vare Trophy over Davies for lowest scoring average by the slenderest of margins, 70.90 to 70.91; Daniel also claimed the Mickey Wright Award for most victories on tour (four).

Davies lost out to Daniel for Rolex Player-of-the-Year honours, but did claim her usual turf, the driving distance crown. She had plenty of chase, however, from Kelly Robbins, a 25 year old American, who won the Jamie Farr Toledo Classic in July, nipping Tammie Green in a play-off following a final round 65. Robbins and Green had fine seasons, cracking the top ten money earners and qualifying for the Solheim Cup squad, where they were paired together.

The year's other major championships fell to Davies at the McDonald's LPGA Championship with rounds of 70-72-69-68; to Patty Sheehan at the US Women's Open on 66-71-69-71 and to Martha Nause at the du Maurier Classic on 65-71-72-71.

Sheehan's win was particularly notable, for several reasons. Firstly, it occurred in an otherwise off-year for the player with one of golf's finest swings. Outside of the Open, Sheehan won only the LPGA Skins Game and posted not a single additional top-three finish. Secondly, Sheehan's Open win was her second in three years, having won at Oakmont in 1992. In the process, she tied the low US Women's Open total of 277. Finally, to win the title, Sheehan had to overcome Helen Alfredsson, who suffered a horrific collapse. Alfredsson opened with a record 63, took a four-shot lead at the halfway point with a 69, then disintegrated over the final 36 holes, closing with 76-77 to finish on one over par, in a sad tie for ninth.

To Alfredsson's enduring credit, she rebounded the following week to win convincingly at Massachusetts; her final round 66 earned her a four-stroke triumph from veterans Pat Bradley and Juli Inkster.

Final, fleeting thoughts must be directed towards Liselotte Neumann, who in 1994 finally fulfilled the promise she showed on her brilliant 1988 US Open victory. Neumann took top honours in a quasi-major, the Weetabix British Open, posted two other US Tour wins, a runner-up, and three third places to go along with an excellent European campaign. Lotte earned more than half a million dollars on the LPGA circuit in 1994. Expect her to build on these successes in 1995.

Donna Andrews (above) and Lotte Neumann shared two Majors and six Tour victories in 1994

THE 1994 LPGA MAJORS

March 24 - 27
NABISCO DINAH SHORE
MISSION HILLS, RANCHO MIRAGE, CALIFORNIA

D Andrews	70	69	67	70	276	$105,000
L Davies	70	68	69	70	277	65,165
T Green	70	72	69	68	279	47,553
J Stephenson	70	69	70	71	280	36,985
M McGann	70	68	70	73	281	29,940
G Graham	73	71	71	68	283	21,251
K Robbins	73	70	69	71	283	21,251
B Burton	73	73	65	72	283	21,251
H Stacy	72	72	70	70	284	15,674
N Lopez	68	72	73	71	284	15,674
M Mallon	72	75	69	69	285	12,064
L Neumann	76	71	68	70	285	12,064

Patty Sheehan won her fifth Major title at Indianwood in July

May 12 - 15
McDONALD'S LPGA CHAMPIONSHIP
DUPONT, WILMINGTON, DELAWARE

L Davies	70	72	69	68	279	$165,000
A Ritzman	68	73	71	70	282	102,402
E Crosby	76	71	69	67	283	54,660
P Bradley	73	73	70	67	283	54,660
H Kobayashi	72	73	71	67	283	54,660
L Neumann	74	73	67	69	283	54,660
S Steinhauer	75	70	72	68	285	27,676
A Alcott	71	75	70	69	285	27,676
B Daniel	72	74	68	71	285	27,676
P Sheehan	72	68	72	73	285	27,676
D Mochrie	68	78	70	70	286	20,203

July 21 - 24
49TH US WOMEN'S OPEN
INDIANWOOD, LAKE OREGON, MICHIGAN

P Sheehan	66	71	69	71	277	$155,000
T Green	66	72	69	71	278	85,000
L Neumann	69	72	71	69	281	47,752
T Abitbol	72	68	73	70	283	31,132
A Alcott	71	67	77	69	284	21,486

M Mallon	70	72	73	69	284	21,486
B King	69	71	72	72	284	21,486
K Robbins	71	72	70	72	285	16,445
D Andrews	67	72	70	76	285	16,445
H Alfredsson	63	69	76	77	285	16,445
L Merten	74	68	75	69	286	12,805
D Mochrie	72	72	71	71	286	12,805
L Davies	68	68	75	75	286	12,805

August 25 - 28
DU MAURIER LTD CLASSIC
OTTAWA HUNT, ONTARIO, CANADA

M Nause	65	71	72	71	279	$120,000
M McGann	66	71	71	72	280	74,474
L Neumann	70	67	71	73	281	54,346
J Geddes	74	67	70	72	283	34,888
M Mallon	70	72	68	73	283	34,888
K Robbins	66	70	73	75	284	20,128
V Fergon	72	68	75	70	285	14,223
S Steinhauer	68	72	73	72	285	14,223
P Sheehan	71	71	68	75	285	14,223
A Alcott	73	70	72	71	286	12,076
D Mochrie	67	74	72	73	286	12,076

THE 1994 LPGA TOUR

TOURNAMENT · WINNERS

HealthSouth Palm Beach Classic	Dawn Coe-Jones	Youngstown-Warren Classic	Tammie Green
Hawaiian Ladies Open	M Figueras-Dotti	Jamie Farr Toledo Classic	Kelly Robbins
Tournament of Champions	Dottie Mochrie	JAL Big Apple Classic	Beth Daniel
Ping/Welch's Championship	Donna Andrews	US Women's Open	Patty Sheehan
Standard Register Ping	Laura Davies	Ping/Welch's Championship	Helen Alfredsson
Nabisco Dinah Shore	Donna Andrews	McCall's Classic	Carolyn Hill
Atlanta Women's Championship	Val Skinner	Weetabix Women's British Open	Liselotte Neumann
Sprint Championship	Sherri Steinhauer	Children's Medical Center Classic	Maggie Will
Sara Lee Classic	Laura Davies	Chicago Challenge	Jane Geddes
McDonald's LPGA Championship	Laura Davies	du Maurier Ltd Classic	Martha Nause
Lady Keystone Open	Elaine Crosby	State Farm Rail Classic	Barb Mucha
Corning Classic	Beth Daniel	Ping-Cellular One Championship	Missie McGeorge
J C Penney LPGA Skins Game	Patty Sheehan	Safeco Classic	Deb Richard
Oldsmobile Classic	Beth Daniel	Heartland Classic	Liselotte Neumann
Minnesota Classic	Liselotte Neumann	World Championship of Women's Golf	Beth Daniel
Rochester International	Lisa Kiggens	Nichirei International	US 22½, Japan 13½
ShopRite Classic	Donna Andrews	Toray Japan Queens Cup	Woo-Soon Ko

LEADING · MONEY · WINNERS

1	Laura Davies	$687,201	18	Judy Dickinson	246,879	34	Michelle Estill	155,667
2	Beth Daniel	659,426	19	Hiromi Kobayashi	242,323	35	Amy Alcott	154,183
3	Liselotte Neumann	505,701	20	Pat Bradley	236,274	36	Barb Mucha	152,685
4	Dottie Mochrie	472,728	21	Dawn Coe-Jones	230,388	37	Colleen Walker	141,200
5	Donna Andrews	429,015	22	Martha Nause	212,130	38	Kristi Albers	136,834
6	Tammie Green	418,969	23	Chris Johnson	208,228	39	Annika Sorenstam	127,451
7	Sherri Steinhauer	413,398	24	Lauri Merten	202,002	40	Gail Graham	124,551
8	Kelly Robbins	396,778	25	Nancy Lopez	197,952	41	Amy Benz	124,189
9	Betsy King	390,239	26	Alicia Dibos	192,132	42	Rosie Jones	123,683
10	Meg Mallon	353,385	27	Nancy Ramsbottom	187,842	43	M Figueras-Dotti	123,513
11	Elaine Crosby	344,735	28	Alice Ritzman	186,715	44	Missie Berteotti	123,161
12	Val Skinner	328,021	29	Lisa Kiggens	183,279	45	Julie Larsen	121,402
13	Patty Sheehan	323,562	30	Missie McGeorge	181,281	46	Carolyn Hill	120,060
14	Helen Alfredsson	277,971	31	Brandie Burton	172,821	47	Joan Pitcock	114,735
15	Jane Geddes	273,600	32	Barbra Bunkowsky	167,039	48	Michelle Redman	113,918
16	Michelle McGann	269,936	33	Dale Eggeling	158,501	49	Juli Inkster	113,829
17	Deb Richard	256,960				50	Kris Tschetter	112,229

1994 SOLHEIM CUP

by Richard Dyson

The theme tune for the 3rd Solheim Cup could have been 'The eyes of the tigress'. The eyes – those piercing eyes, belonged to irrepressible American Dottie Mochrie, scourge of the Europeans. The 29 year old New Yorker had been inconsolable in defeat two years earlier and was desperate for revenge. In the luxurious confines of The Greenbrier, resplendent in the colours of the West Virginian fall, she got it. Mochrie drove the US fans dotty with delight, for, as they fervently waved the Stars and Stripes, she was the Star in Stripes; the tigress (with fitting flame-red hair) who stalked her European prey and then mauled it mercilessly. While it was hardly a one-woman show (her partner 'in crime', Brandie Burton also finished with three wins out of three) there's no doubting that fiery Dottie took on the inspirational role that Europe had hoped Laura Davies would play.

Mochrie's passion merely emphasised the great strides made by the Solheim Cup in its short history, making it now, indisputably, the biggest event in women's golf. With honours even, after a convincing 11½ – 4½ US win at Lake Nona in 1990, followed by a sensational 11½ – 6½ European riposte in Scotland in 1992, the clash at The Greenbrier was looked upon as 'the decider'.

Pumped-up and patriotic: Dottie Mochrie at The Greenbrier

Desperate to avenge their Dalmahoy disappointment, with home advantage and led by their fiercely competitive golfing legend, JoAnne Carner, the Americans were never going to lack motivation. In terms of talent, they were also formidable, boasting 20 major titles between them to Europe's eight. Their greater strength in depth (Carner could afford to overlook such 'greats' as Lopez and Bradley for her one wild card selection, Kelly Robbins) was also more suited to the format change, at their instigation, which would see each team member playing every day.

Saturday (won 3-2 by the US).

Carner's trump cards were Burton and Mochrie, who led from the front on both days and claimed the prized scalps of Alfredsson and Neumann on Friday and then, crucially, those 'Euro bankers' Davies and Nicholas, in 'the clash of the titans' on Saturday. The only other one hundred per cent successful pairing – and what a delightful bonus for Mickey Walker – was the combination of Europe's gritty Scot, Dale Reid and 'the baby-faced killer' from Lancashire, Lora Fairclough, a revelation on her Solheim Cup debut. They twice saw off Green

Helen Alfredsson and Lotte Neumann flew the European flag (metaphorically speaking) when they won an epic fourball match against Patty Sheehan and Sherri Steinhauer

However, Europe, led for the third time by Mickey Walker, could claim to possess greater Solheim Cup experience, with just two rookies as opposed to the home nation's four. Theirs was a familiar and settled side (comprising four Swedes, four English and two Scots) and known to have great team spirit. Also, in Davies and Neumann, it included the world's number one and number two ranked players.

After the first two riveting days there was nothing in it. Both captains kept faith with the same pairings for the foursomes on Friday (won 3-2 by Europe) and the fourballs on

and Robbins, recording in the fourballs the visitors' biggest win (5 & 3) in the contest.

The two closest matches involved the Swedes (Sweden I: 'Alfie' and Lotta, and Sweden II: Catrin and Annika), and, importantly for Europe, were won on the final green. On Friday Nilsmark holed a crucial three footer to defeat the strong US pairing of Daniel and Mallon – who duly gained their revenge, with the event's biggest win of 7 & 5, the following day. However, the whole balance of the first two days rested on the final putt on Saturday, a pressure-packed four footer, holed

Lancashire's
Lora Fairclough
was a revelation
at The
Greenbrier

by 'Alfie', to defeat Sheehan and Steinhauer and level the match at 5-5.

So, the stage was perfectly set for Sunday's final 10 singles, which both teams could approach with optimism – Europe on a psychological 'up' after 'Alfie's' putt and knowing that five points would retain the Cup – the US, believing (correctly as it turned out) that their individual strength would see them clinch the necessary 5½ points to regain the trophy.

In the end it all proved very one-sided as

America swept to a crushing 8-2 singles victory (only King and Sheehan were defeated, by Alfredsson and Nicholas, respectively). The entire contest produced no halved matches and, once again, on Sunday Dottie Mochrie produced no half-measures, as she set the trend for the day. Though playing in the second singles, hers was the first point posted, as she annihilated 1992 heroine Catrin Nilsmark by 6 & 5, with a stunning display of golf (seven under par through 13 holes).

Fittingly, it was Meg Mallon, whose loss to Nilsmark at Dalmahoy had signalled defeat for America, who had the honour of claiming the decisive point when she beat Pam Wright by two holes. Captain Carner was overcome, while a visibly deflated Laura Davies went down, as Brandie Burton gained revenge for her 1992 top singles defeat by the Englishwoman.

The 3rd Solheim Cup provided more than a hint of déjà vu for European golf: fifteen years earlier at The Greenbrier, in the Ryder Cup, the visitors had been neck and neck with their hosts over the first two days before being 'put to the sword' in the singles. The pattern was repeated this time, with the margin of defeat (17-11 in 1979, 13-7 in 1994) being once again six points.

The moment
of victory:
Meg Mallon is
embraced by
her jubilant
team mates
as the United
States wins
back the
Solheim Cup

The ultimate prize in women's golf: Karsten Solheim presents US captain JoAnne Carner with the Solheim Cup trophy

THE 3RD SOLHEIM CUP

21-23 October, The Greenbrier, White Sulphur Springs, West Virginia

Foursomes

B Burton & D Mochrie bt H Alfredsson & L Neumann 3 & 2
B Daniel & M Mallon lost to C Nilsmark & A Sorenstam 1 hole
T Green & K Robbins lost to L Fairclough & D Reid 2 & 1
D Andrews & B King lost to L Davies & A Nicholas 2 & 1
P Sheehan & S Steinhauer bt T Johnson & P Wright 2 holes
FOURSOMES: USA 2 EUROPE 3

Fourballs

B Burton & D Mochrie bt L Davies & A Nicholas 2 & 1
B Daniel & M Mallon bt C Nilsmark & A Sorenstam 7 & 5
T Green & K Robbins lost to L Fairclough & D Reid 5 & 3
D Andrews & B King bt T Johnson & P Wright 3 & 2
P Sheehan & S Steinhauer lost to H Alfredsson & L Neumann 1 hole
FOURBALLS: USA 3 EUROPE 2

Singles

B King lost to H Alfredsson 2 & 1
D Mochrie bt C Nilsmark 6 & 5
B Daniel bt T Johnson 2 holes
K Robbins bt L Fairclough 4 & 2
M Mallon bt P Wright 2 holes
P Sheehan lost to A Nicholas 3 & 2
B Burton bt L Davies 2 holes
T Green bt A Sorenstam 3 & 2
S Steinhauer bt D Reid 2 holes
D Andrews bt L Neumann 3 & 2
SINGLES: USA 8 EUROPE 2

FINAL SCORE: USA 13 EUROPE 7

AUSTRALASIA

1994 AUSTRALASIAN TOUR REVIEW

According to the Chinese, 1994 was the Year of the Dog. Down Under
on the Australasian golf tour, it was the year of the underdog

The pattern was set in the year's first tournament, the AMP New Zealand Open in January when Kiwi Frank Nobilo was denied a popular home victory by 24 year old Australian Craig Jones. It was the third time Nobilo had finished runner-up in his native championship.

The Tour then headed for Victoria where Melbourne's Robert Allenby was the favourite to retain his Players Championship title at Kingston Heath – and if not Allenby, surely Craig Parry or Peter Senior? The winner was Patrick Burke, a 31 year old American who'd never won a professional tournament before.

It wasn't just a case of shock winners – although there were plenty more of those to come – but shocking, unexpected conclusions to tournaments that were also such a feature in 1994. In the second half of the season the back nine drama of the Heineken Australian Open

From near-victory at The Vines to near-disaster at Royal Melbourne, 1994 was an extraordinary year for Robert Allenby

and Dunhill Asian Masters events provided the most striking examples, but as early as the third event of the year, the Heineken Classic at The Vines, Murphy's Law was in evidence.

With Ian Woosnam surprisingly missing the cut, Allenby was again the man to beat and turning for home on the final day, he shared the lead with Wayne Smith. But at the 10th hole Australia's rising star incurred a two stroke penalty for inadvertently improving his lie in a

Masters win (and second Gold Jacket).

There was one more tournament before the lengthy 'winter' break, and one more dramatic finish when Peter Senior birdied the final hole in the Canon Challenge to force a play-off with Chris Gray, then promptly birdied the first sudden-death hole to defeat his stunned opponent.

When the Tour recommenced in October, the promising 25 year old Lucas Parsons

A showdown between Ernie Els and Greg Norman was anticipated at Huntingdale
but it was Craig Parry who eventually triumphed

hazard. It took the wind from his sails, whereupon Mike Clayton became the main challenger to Smith and, with a birdie at the final hole, secured his victory.

Tieing with Allenby for third place behind Clayton and Smith at The Vines was Pat Burke. And he was in the news again a fortnight later in the Australian Masters at Huntingdale. Burke shared the lead after 36 holes with rounds of 69-71 which was seven strokes ahead of the six-time champion Greg Norman. The other joint leader was Ernie Els, making his Australian Masters debut. The South African forged ahead in the third round and was most people's choice to win on Sunday. It didn't happen, however, not because Els played poorly, but because Craig Parry shot a superb five under par 68, enabling him to seize his second

captured the Foodlink Queensland Open, edging out the even more promising Michael Campbell while Burma's Kyi Hla Han got the better of Wayne Grady in the Epson Singapore Open at Tanah Merah.

Time for a big-name winner? Given the quality of the field that assembled in Bali for the inaugural Alfred Dunhill Asian Masters, it seemed highly probable that one would now emerge. Sure enough, with brilliant rounds of 67-63-69, Nick Faldo was cruising to a first Australasian Tour victory. Six strokes ahead with six to play the only thing that could stop him from winning was.... disqualification. Another rules infringement! This time it was the moving of a piece of coral from a bunker – permissible on the European Tour but not on the Australasian Tour. Canadian Jack Kay won

The Tour
visited several
outstanding
venues in 1994
and none more
glorious than
the New South
Wales Golf Club
at Botany Bay

in Faldo's absence and *Golf Weekly* magazine ran the headline, 'Faldo Wrecked on Coral Grief'.

Seven days later, and the Tour having returned to Australia, our American friend Pat Burke was leading the Order of Merit after his second win of the season in the Victorian Open. Next came Sydney and a visit to the spectacular New South Wales Golf Club. With its location on Botany Bay, perhaps it was

appropriate – or ironic – that a British golfer should win the Australian PGA Championship there. Scotland's Andrew Coltart achieved the biggest win of his short career by overcoming strong winds and a double-bogey at his first hole on Sunday to record a two shot triumph.

So far on the '94 Tour we had seen exciting finishes, surprising winners and a shocking disqualification; now came the Heineken

Australian Open. It is reviewed in detail ahead, suffice to say here that the conclusion at Royal Sydney was at once exciting, surprising and shocking! It also gave the Tour a new Order of Merit leader. By capturing the season's biggest prize, Robert Allenby leap-frogged to the top of the Money List.

Allenby was still in front after the Greg Norman Holden Classic at Royal Melbourne. This was the event that finally confirmed 1994

the penultimate event, the Air New Zealand Shell Open at The Grange, all that remained was for Burke to snatch the Order of Merit crown from under Allenby's nose in the Coolum Classic. As Allenby's nose was in Jamaica at the time it seemed possible, but fortunately for the Australian (and for Australian pride) Mike Clayton emerged as the winner, thus securing a Vines – Coolum resort double.

Champions in Melbourne, Perth and Sydney. From left to right: Craig Parry, Mike Clayton and Andrew Coltart

as the year of the underdog – thanks to the Shark. Sharing the lead with nine holes of his 'own' tournament to play, Norman went head-to-head with Anthony Gilligan – and lost.

With 'unknown' Shane Robinson winning

It was Clayton, remember, who had benefited most from Allenby's aberration at the Heineken Classic in January. At Coolum in December, 'Claytes' repaid the debt with interest.

American Patrick Burke came close to winning the 1994 Australasian Order of Merit.

HEINEKEN AUSTRALIAN OPEN

ROLL · OF · HONOUR

YEAR	WINNER
1904	Michael Scott (Am)
1905	Dan Soutar
1906	Carnegie Clark
1907	Michael Scott (Am)
1908	Clyde Pearce (Am)
1909	Claude Felstead (Am)
1910	Carnegie Clark
1911	Carnegie Clark
1912	Ivo Whitton (Am)
1913	Ivo Whitton (Am)
1914-19	no championship
1920	Joe Kirkwood
1921	Arthur Le Fevre
1922	Charles Campbell
1923	Tom Howard
1924	Alex Russell (Am)
1925	Fred Popplewell
1926	Ivo Whitton (Am)
1927	Rufus Stewart
1928	Fred Popplewell
1929	Ivo Whitton (Am)
1930	Francis Eyre
1931	Ivo Whitton (Am)
1932	Mick Ryan (Am)
1933	Lou Kelly
1934	Bill Bolger
1935	F W McMahon
1936	Gene Sarazen
1937	George Naismith
1938	Jim Ferrier (Am)
1939	Jim Ferrier (Am)
1940-45	no championship
1946	Ossie Pickworth
1947	Ossie Pickworth
1948	Ossie Pickworth
1949	Eric Cremin
1950	Norman von Nida
1951	Peter Thomson
1952	Norman von Nida
1953	Norman von Nida
1954	Ossie Pickworth
1955	Bobby Locke
1956	Bruce Crampton
1957	Frank Phillips
1958	Gary Player
1959	Kel Nagle
1960	Bruce Devlin (Am)
1961	Frank Phillips
1962	Gary Player
1963	Gary Player
1964	Jack Nicklaus
1965	Gary Player
1966	Arnold Palmer
1967	Peter Thomson
1968	Jack Nicklaus
1969	Gary Player
1970	Gary Player
1971	Jack Nicklaus
1972	Peter Thomson
1973	J C Snead
1974	Gary Player
1975	Jack Nicklaus
1976	Jack Nicklaus
1977	David Graham
1978	Jack Nicklaus
1979	Jack Newton
1980	Greg Norman
1981	Bill Rogers
1982	Bob Shearer
1983	Peter Fowler
1984	Tom Watson
1985	Greg Norman
1986	Rodger Davis
1987	Greg Norman
1988	Mark Calcavecchia
1989	Peter Senior
1990	John Morse
1991	Wayne Riley
1992	Steve Elkington
1993	Brad Faxon
1994	Robert Allenby

Three-time champion Greg Norman finished joint fourth at Royal Sydney in 1994

1994 HEINEKEN AUSTRALIAN OPEN

'No race is ever over 'til the last yard's run
No game is ever lost until it's won
No fire is ever dead whilst the ashes are still red
Nor the sun set in the skies until the day is done'

In November 1991 a 20 year old amateur waited beside the 18th green at Royal Melbourne, wondering if he was about to win the Australian Open. He had just birdied the final hole after hitting an arrow-straight 5-iron to within two feet of the flag – a shot reminiscent of Jerry Pate's brilliant stroke at the 72nd hole in the 1976 US Open. Robert Allenby was five years' old then. But now he held his breath as Wayne Riley walked on to the 18th green. Riley had birdied the 16th and 17th holes to draw level with Allenby, but his approach had left him with a putt of at least 40 feet. Moments later Riley was

running across the green, punching the air in delight. A third successive birdie had defeated the prodigy from Melbourne. He would have to wait and wonder a little longer.

Three years later a similar scene was being enacted. This time it was at Royal Sydney rather than Royal Melbourne, and the player approaching the 18th green was Brett Ogle. But once again it was the Heineken Australian Open and the young man waiting beside the green was Robert Allenby, now 23 years old and one of the most promising professional golfers in the world.

Allenby had completed his round on eight under par, Ogle was also eight under, although he needed to hole a ten foot putt to remain so and force a play-off. Ogle studied his putt carefully, took aim and missed. Allenby had fulfilled his destiny.

It is a nice tale but what it doesn't reveal is the extent of the drama that took place at Royal Sydney on that November day last year.

From the outset the 1994 Heineken Australian Open was a good championship but it evolved into a great one.

For once Greg Norman didn't play a prominent role in the proceedings. Certainly, he was present at Royal Sydney but when play began he seemed to have other things on his mind – World Tours for instance – and his opening scores of 74-70 left him with too much ground to make up at the weekend. Typically, the Shark gave it his best shot and he eventually finished tied for fourth, but he couldn't hole enough putts to threaten the leaders on the final day.

For much of the week Ogle was the front runner. He was one stroke behind Matthew King after a 69 in the first round, then took the lead on Friday with a superbly fashioned 68: 'the best golf I have played from tee to green all year.' He also told the world's media that he was feeling especially relaxed following a 'beautiful month spent fishing and camping'!

Australian golfers monopolised the top five places on the leaderboard after 36 holes. Ogle was on 137 (seven under par), one ahead of Wayne Grady (70-68) and two in front of the Australian Masters champion Craig Parry and Jeff Woodland, runner-up in the 1993 Heineken Australian Open at Metropolitan. Next came Allenby on 140 (70-70).

What had happened to the overseas threat? The defending champion, American Brad Faxon began well enough with a 70 but slipped to a

Robert Allenby launches one down the middle. For 14 holes on Sunday he could do no wrong

76 in the second round. Like Norman, he rallied over the weekend but again, by then it was too late. His fellow countryman, Mark Calcavecchia, winner of the Australian Open when it was last staged at Royal Sydney in 1988, scored a 74 in the first round but recovered with a fine 67 on Friday. At the half-way stage Calcavecchia was four behind Ogle and leading the international challenge alongside England's Peter Baker and the Frenchman Jean Van de Velde.

On Saturday Ogle increased his lead to two strokes with another very solid round of 70. He was, he assured us, still very relaxed but equally, very determined: 'To win this championship would mean as much to me as winning a Major', he declared.

Behind him a posse of players was lying in wait. Ogle had advanced his score to nine under par (207); Peter Baker and New Zealander Paul Davenport now shared second place on seven under par, with Allenby, after a third successive round of 70 on six under. Four strokes behind Ogle were the potentially

(Above) Brett Ogle's putt refuses to drop at the final hole. (Right) Peter Baker finished third on his Open debut

dangerous duo of Peter Senior and Craig Parry and on four under par, five off the pace were Greg Norman and Mark Calcavecchia.

Of course, to have any chance of winning, the players 'lying in wait' needed either a fast start on Sunday or a collapse from Ogle.

For the first 14 holes of the final round Ogle played just as well as he had played on Thursday, Friday and Saturday. He took his score from nine under to 10 under for the championship. Yet he had lost his lead.

During his first 14 holes on Sunday Robert Allenby appeared to be playing a different course from everyone else. While Parry, Calcavecchia and Senior were on their way to compiling scores of 76, 79 and 81 respectively (it was fairly breezy) Allenby was seven under par for his round. In those 14 holes he had five birdies and one eagle.

At 13 under par, three ahead of Ogle – and the rest of the field nowhere in sight – Allenby looked unstoppable. Suddenly things started to go wrong: he bogeyed the 15th, but it didn't seem to matter as Ogle, playing directly behind him, followed suit. Then at the 16th he ran up a double bogey seven; Ogle parred the hole to be just one behind. Allenby bogeyed the 17th; amazingly Ogle did likewise. If Destiny was waiting behind the 18th green for the young Melbourne golfer she was playing cruel tricks: Allenby bogeyed the 18th – his fifth dropped stroke in four holes! But even crueller tricks were being played on Brett Ogle and when his 10 foot putt for a par slipped past the cup Allenby was the champion.

Now Destiny owes Brett Ogle.

November 24 - 27
HEINEKEN AUSTRALIAN OPEN
ROYAL SYDNEY, NSW

R Allenby	70	70	70	70	280	Aus$153,000
B Ogle	69	68	70	74	281	86,700
P Baker	70	71	68	73	282	57,375
B Faxon	70	76	67	70	283	35,133
G Orr	76	68	68	71	283	35,133
G Norman	74	70	68	71	283	35,133
D Bransdon	69	73	70	72	284	Am.
P Devenport	73	69	67	75	284	27,200
W Grady	70	68	74	73	285	22,950
L Stephen	73	69	70	73	285	22,950
P Moloney	70	72	70	73	285	22,950
P Fulke	73	71	73	69	286	15,810
M Weir	76	69	69	72	286	15,810
J Woodland	70	69	72	75	286	15,810
M Harwood	73	71	70	72	286	15,810
G Chalmers	73	72	66	75	286	Am.
S Owen	74	71	75	67	287	10,178
P O'Malley	75	72	70	70	287	10,178
G Waite	73	70	72	72	287	10,178
M Clayton	75	67	70	75	287	10,178
A Bruyns	70	74	71	72	287	10,178
C Parry	70	69	72	76	287	10,178

THE 1994 AUSTRALASIAN TOUR

January 27 - 30
HEINEKEN CLASSIC
THE VINES, PERTH

M Clayton	67	71	71	70	279	Aus$54,000
W Smith	69	67	73	73	282	20,800
P Burke	68	68	78	69	283	17,325
R Allenby	70	69	71	73	283	17,325
D Ecob	72	70	75	67	284	12,000
C Van der Velde	67	72	73	73	285	10,800
J Senior	71	77	70	68	286	9,250
R Green	70	70	75	71	286	9,250
M Campbell	73	67	78	69	287	7,050
J Senden	68	74	72	73	287	7,050
R Gibson	70	70	73	74	287	7,050
T Herron	70	70	70	77	287	7,050

February 17 - 20
MICROSOFT AUSTRALIAN MASTERS
HUNTINGDALE, MELBOURNE

C Parry	74	70	70	68	282	Aus$135,000
E Els	70	70	72	73	285	76,500
P Senior	73	71	74	68	286	43,312
P Teravainen	71	70	75	70	286	43,312
W Smith	71	74	72	70	287	30,000
R Willis	74	72	73	69	288	23,250
M Harwood	69	76	71	72	288	23,250
W Grady	68	75	72	73	288	23,250
L Parsons	74	71	71	72	288	23,250

November 17 - 20
REEBOK AUSTRALIAN PGA CHAMPIONSHIP
NEW SOUTH WALES GC, SYDNEY

A Coltart	67	67	77	70	281	Aus$36,000
T Price	67	73	72	71	283	20,400
M Harwood	69	69	72	74	284	13,500
G Moorhead	67	73	73	72	285	8,800
W Riley	70	71	72	72	285	8,800
P Moloney	69	71	73	73	286	6,467
E Boult	64	71	78	73	286	6,467
P Devenport	66	69	73	78	286	6,467

TOURNAMENT · WINNERS

AMP New Zealand Open	Craig Jones
Optus Players Championship	Pat Burke
Heineken Classic	Mike Clayton
Microsoft Australian Masters	Craig Parry
Canon Challenge	Peter Senior
Foodlink Queensland Open	Lucas Parsons
Epson Singapore Open	Kyi Hla Han
Alfred Dunhill Asian Masters	Jack Kay
Victorian Open	Pat Burke
Reebok Australian PGA	Andrew Coltart
Heineken Australian Open	Robert Allenby
Greg Norman's Holden Classic	Anthony Gilligan
Air New Zealand Shell Open	Shane Robinson
Coolum Classic	Mike Clayton

1994 ORDER OF MERIT: TOP 25

1	Robert Allenby	Aus$199,6445
2	Craig Parry	185,920
3	Patrick Burke	182,571
4	Mike Clayton	177,663
5	Anthony Gilligan	136,327
6	Wayne Grady	128,896
7	Peter Senior	125,531
8	Lucas Parsons	103,828
9	Paul Moloney	99,397
10	Andre Stolz	91,525
11	Chris Gray	91,156
12	Jack Kay	89,716
13	Robert Willis	88,104
14	Terry Price	84,754
15	Paul Devenport	79,217
16	Mike Harwood	70,420
17	Michael Campbell	65,132
18	Craig Jones	59,105
19	Jack O'Keefe	58,274
20	Shane Robinson	57,868
21	Peter Teravainen	56,412
22	Peter O'Malley	49,296
23	Simon Owen	48,798
24	Peter Fowler	47,870
25	Bradley Hughes	46,984

JAPAN

1994 JAPANESE TOUR REVIEW

**The whispers were beginning to grow louder: Japan's greatest ever player
was no longer the force he had once been**

For the best part of two decades and especially since the late 1980s, Masashi 'Jumbo' Ozaki had reigned supreme. Arguably his finest year had occurred as recently as 1992, when he won six tournaments including his fourth Japan Open Championship. But 1993 had been very disappointing. He won twice early in the season but then a succession of final day collapses proved very costly – including the loss of the Japanese Open title and the Order of Merit crown. The lacklustre way he began 1994 only gave further ammunition to the purveyors of doom and decline.

In the first Japanese tournament of 1994 an 'unknown' New Zealander, Craig Warren got the better of Jumbo in the final round to win the Token Corporation Cup. True, Jumbo claimed the Dunlop Open at the end of April (officially an Asian Tour event, although staged in Japan) but the player who dominated the early part of the season was Ozaki's old rival, Tommy Nakajima who won three of the first ten events. Jumbo didn't win again until the Yonex Hiroshima tournament in mid July, the Tour by then having completed approximately half of its schedule.

A third success came at the end of the summer (September's ANA Open) but Ozaki was still being overshadowed – not now by Nakajima, whose form had deserted him, but by the brilliant play of American Brian Watts,

(Left) American David Ishii won twice on the 1994 Tour. (Right) 'Jet' Naomichi and 'Jumbo' Masashi Ozaki

Barry Lane drives at the Dunlop Phoenix Tournament in November. The English golfer featured prominently but had no answer to Jumbo's final round 65

winner of the 1993 Asian Order of Merit. Watts won his third Japanese tournament of the year in September and a month later captured the Bridgestone Open (overcoming Nick Price among others) and the Philip Morris Championship in consecutive weeks. Now for Jumbo's response...

At the age of 47, perhaps it was time to ease up a little and allow a younger player to bask in the limelight – an appropriate place for somebody called Watts? No chance. Jumbo didn't only fight back (and silence all the whispers) but he produced, incredibly, the finest golf of his life.

At the beginning of October Jumbo stormed to a thirteen stroke victory in the Japan Open at Yokkaichi, regaining his title with rounds of 68-66-69-67 for a record score of 270 (18 under par). Five weeks later he compiled an identical four-round total in the Daiwa International at Hatoyama Country Club. On this occasion scores of 65-72-70-63 were good enough to secure a massive fifteen stroke winning margin!

Now came the start of the International Tour – Japan's 'festival of golf', comprising three lucrative tournaments which traditionally attract strong international fields. Seve Ballesteros, Phil Mickelson and Craig Parry were among the entrants for the 1994 Visa Taiheiyo Masters where, in the shadows of Mount Fuji, Jumbo Ozaki duly won his sixth event of the year. Thus he had surpassed Brian Watts' haul of victories and matched his feat of winning back-to-back tournaments. Now for seven wins and three in a row.

The Dunlop Phoenix is Japan's richest tournament: past winners include Ballesteros (twice), Johnny Miller, Graham Marsh, Tom Watson and (in 1993) Ernie Els. The 1994 tournament was its 21st staging; the field was especially strong – but Jumbo Ozaki was strong enough. With a final round of 65 (the lowest ever by a champion) he overtook a rejuvenated Tom Watson and finished in style with a birdie at the 72nd hole.

What a year! A White Jacket for winning the Asian Tour's Dunlop Open and a Scarlet Blazer for capturing the Visa Taiheiyo Masters; a fifth Japan Open; a sixth Order of Merit title and the first player to win over two hundred million Yen in a season. 'Call me the Japanese George Foreman', he said. More like the Japanese Muhammad Ali.

JAPAN'S 1994 INTERNATIONAL TOUR

November 10 -13
SUMITOMO VISA TAIHEIYO MASTERS
TAIHEIYO CLUB, SHIZUOKA PREFECTURE

M Ozaki	66	69	68	67	270	Y27,000,000
B Estes	68	67	72	68	275	15,000,000
C Parry	68	69	75	64	276	7,200,000
K Murota	71	68	70	67	276	7,200,000
E Mizoguchi	70	67	71	68	276	7,200,000
Y Mizumaki	69	70	67	70	276	7,200,000
T Nakajima	67	71	73	66	277	4,350,000
L Mize	67	70	72	68	277	4,350,000
D Ishii	70	71	66	70	277	4,350,000
T Hamilton	69	70	71	68	278	3,450,000
H Kase	75	69	69	66	279	2,760,000
S Maruyama	68	74	67	70	279	2,760,000
E Itai	70	69	67	73	279	2,760,000
I Shirahama	68	73	71	68	280	1,992,000
P Mickelson	69	71	72	68	280	1,992,000
S Ballesteros	73	69	70	68	280	1,992,000
T Nakamura	72	69	68	71	280	1,992,000
K Tomori	71	67	69	73	280	1,992,000

The 'Jumbo Tour': last Autumn Masashi Ozaki was invincible.

S Higashi	67	71	70	208	2,250,000
B Watts	72	68	69	209	1,660,000
E Mizoguchi	72	67	70	209	1,660,000
E Els	66	73	70	209	1,660,000
P Senior	73	65	71	209	1,660,000
L Nelson	68	70	71	209	1,660,000
C Rocca	71	66	72	209	1,660,000

November 17 - 20
DUNLOP PHOENIX TOURNAMENT
PHOENIX, MAYAZAKI

M Ozaki	67	69	65	201	Y27,000,000
T Watson	66	68	68	202	15,000,000
S Hoch	71	69	64	204	7,800,000
N Serizawa	69	66	69	204	7,800,000
B Lane	66	69	69	204	7,800,000
L Mize	68	71	66	205	5,100,000
N Ozaki	68	68	69	205	5,100,000
I Aoki	71	67	68	206	4,125,000
D Ishii	71	65	70	206	4,125,000
Y Mizumari	69	70	68	207	2,932,000
K Idoki	68	71	68	207	2,932,000
T Lehman	68	71	68	207	2,932,000
M A Jimenez	72	67	68	207	2,932,000
M Kimura	70	71	67	208	2,250,000

November 24 - 27
CASIO WORLD OPEN
IBUSUKI KAIMON, KAGOSHIMA

R Gamez	68	66	68	69	271	Y27,000,000
S Hoch	70	69	67	69	275	15,000,000
J M Olazabal	70	70	70	67	277	8,700,000
E Mizoguchi	73	66	67	71	277	8,700,000
B Watts	69	73	71	65	278	5,700,000
S Ikeuchi	70	65	74	69	278	5,700,000
M Kusakabe	73	70	69	67	279	3,900,000
Y Nuseki	70	74	67	68	279	3,900,000
C S Hsieh	71	68	71	69	279	3,900,000
S Higashi	69	70	70	70	279	3,900,000
W Smith	67	69	68	75	279	3,900,000
R Gibson	69	69	73	69	280	2,540,000
H Kase	74	69	67	70	280	2,540,000
M Kawamura	69	70	71	71	280	2,540,000

1994 PGA JAPAN TOUR

TOURNAMENT · WINNERS

Token Corporation Cup	Craig Warren
DyoDo Drinco Shizuoka Open	Tommy Nakajima
United KSB Setonaikai Open	Kazuhiro Takami
Descente Classic Cup	Brian Watts
Pocari Sweat Open	Yoshinori Mizumaki
Tsuruya Open	Tommy Nakajima
The Crowns	Roger MacKay
Fujisankei Classic	Kiyoshi Murota
Japan PGA Championship	Hiroshi Goda
Pepsi Ube Tournament	Tommy Nakajima
Mitsubishi Galant	Katsuyoshi Tomori
JCB Classic Sendai	Masahiro Kuramoto
Sapporo Tokyu Open	Yoshinori Mizumaki
Yomiuri Open	Tsukasa Watanabe
Mizuno Open	Brian Watts
Japan PGA Philanthropy	Todd Hamilton
Yonex Open Hiroshima	Masashi Ozaki
Nikkei Cup	Torakichi Nakamura
Memorial	Toru Suzuki
NST Niigate Open	Pete Izumikawa
ACOM International	Naomichi Ozaki
Maruman Open	David Ishii
Hisamitsu KBC Augusta	Brian Watts
JPGA Matchplay Championship	Todd Hamilton
Suntory Open	David Ishii
ANA Open	Masashi Ozaki
Gene Sarazen Jun Classic	Carlos Franco
Japan Open Golf Championship	Masashi Ozaki
Tokai Classic	Corey Pavin
Asahi Beer Golf Digest	Eiji Mizoguchi
Bridgestone Open	Brian Watts
Philip Morris Golf Championship	Brian Watts
Daiwa International	Masashi Ozaki
Sumitomo Visa Taheiyo Masters	Masashi Ozaki
Dunlop Phoenix	Masashi Ozaki
Casio World Open	Robert Gamez
Japan Series	Hisayuki Sasaki
Daikyo Open	Hideki Kase

LEADING · MONEY · WINNERS

1	Masashi Ozaki	Y215,468,000
2	Brian Watts	139,052,710
3	Tsuneyuki Nakajima	115,771,280
4	Naomichi Ozaki	91,685,057
5	David Ishii	87,271,410
6	Todd Hamilton	86,960,890
7	Eiji Mizoguchi	79,771,083
8	Hisayuki Sasaki	77,077,194
9	Nobuo Serizawa	69,619,200
10	Tsukasa Watanabe	65,455,698
11	Kiyoshi Murota	63,222,505
12	Masahiro Kuramoto	62,655,316
13	Hideki Kase	59,781,084
14	Yoshinori Mizumaki	56,076,556
15	Katsuyoshi Tomori	54,921,414
16	Yoshinori Kaneko	53,695,686
17	Masayuki Kawamura	52,867,173
18	Roger MacKay	49,896,904
19	Hsieh Chin-Sheng	49,243,852
20	Hiroshi Ueda	44,524,800

Brian Watts

SOUTH AFRICA

1993-1994 SOUTH AFRICAN TOUR REVIEW

T.J. was on a roll, and not even the best golfers in the world could stop him

Tony Johnstone would be the first to admit that he neither looks nor swings a club remotely like Ernie Els. A man of modest height and build, he has a golf swing that purrs as smoothly as.... a well-oiled tractor.

But why should that bother him? It was Johnstone, not Els, who ruled the fairways in South Africa last year. He seized the South African Order of Merit crown from fellow Zimbabwean Mark McNulty with consummate ease and won three tournaments. During one

purple patch the quality of his play was nothing less than sensational.

The First National Bank Tour runs from November to February and follows the South African summer. (The Million Dollar Challenge, won by Nick Price in 1993 and Nick Faldo in 1994 is regarded as a 'non Order of Merit' tournament). Price, Els, and David Frost all made sporadic Tour appearances and, at varying times, each was eclipsed by Johnstone. Price (and, of course, McNulty) played in the Zimbabwean Open, which Johnstone won by

Mark McNulty and Tony Johnstone refuse to be overshadowed by Messrs Price and Els

remarkable 61 en route to retaining his ICL International title by eight strokes.

The most emotional win of the 1993-1994 season was achieved by perennial bridesmaid, Chris Davison, who captured his first Tour victory, the South African Masters at the end of January. The English born Davison finally discovered the secret of winning at the Lost City Golf Club. 'This is an unbelievable feeling,' he said, 'One I can savour forever'. And not even the resort's famous crocodiles were going to spoil his party.

David Frost (Left) and Nick Price both won on the South African Tour early in 1994

eight shots; Els came a distant second to him in the South African Open while Frost and Els shared second place behind Johnstone in the Bells Cup. For those three tournaments – and they were successive Order of Merit events – the Zimbabwean was 53 under par. His play in the South African Open, staged at the Durban Country Club was especially brilliant, as he compiled rounds of 64-69-69-65 to win by seven shots with a championship record score of 21 under par.

If Johnstone cooled a little in the second half of the season it was only to be expected. He nearly claimed the final event of the 1993-1994 season, however, the Mount Edgecombe Trophy, where he was beaten in a play-off by Bruce Vaughan, the American holing a 25 foot putt on the final green of regulation play.

So Johnstone wasn't totally dominant. Nor did he have a monopoly in the art of low scoring and runaway victories. McNulty was most impressive in winning the FNB Players Championship by five strokes at Royal Johannesburg; Frost stormed home nine clear of the field with a 21 under par total in the Lexington PGA Championship at the Wanderers Golf Club and a week later Price opened with a

SOUTH AFRICAN TOUR SUMMARY

1993-1994
SOUTH AFRICAN TOUR

TOURNAMENT · WINNERS

FNB Players Championship	Mark McNulty
Zimbabwe Open	Tony Johnstone
1993 Million Dollar Challenge	Nick Price
South African Open	Tony Johnstone
Bells Cup	Tony Johnstone
Lexington PGA Championship	David Frost
ICL International	Nick Price
South African Masters	Chris Davison
Hollard Swazi Classic	Omar Uresti
Mount Edgecombe Trophy	Bruce Vaughan

ORDER OF MERIT

1	Tony Johnstone	Rand297,358
2	Bruce Vaughan	189,452
3	Ernie Els	160,410
4	Chris Davison	156,219
5	Roger Wessels	135,517
6	Wayne Westner	127,423
7	Ben Fouchee	107,612
8	John Bland	87,781
9	Ian Leggatt	78,404
10	Omar Uresti	76,675

Tony Johnstone enjoyed spectacular success on the FNB Tour.

Nick Faldo, winner of the 1994 Million Dollar Challenge.

December 1 - 4
1994 NEDBANK MILLION DOLLAR CHALLENGE
GARY PLAYER CC, SUN CITY

N Faldo	66	64	73	69	272	$1,000,000
N Price	71	66	70	68	275	250,000
E Els	68	70	67	72	277	187,500
D Frost	73	67	71	66	277	187,500
B Langer	68	69	74	68	279	137,500
T Lehman	71	69	70	69	279	137,500
S Ballesteros	76	71	68	66	281	110,000
M McNulty	72	69	68	73	282	100,000
C Pavin	71	70	72	70	283	100,000
H Irwin	72	70	74	72	288	100,000
C Montgomerie	72	71	72	73	288	100,000
V Singh	80	73	76	78	307	100,000

1994 MILLION DOLLAR CHALLENGE

It was very hot. Nick Faldo was sporting a white cap and Fanny was wearing sun glasses – apart from that it was just like Muirfield. In the Open Championship two and a half years earlier, Faldo scored 66-64-69-73 for a famous, and ultimately thrilling victory. At Sun City last December Nick scored 66-64-73-69 for a memorable, and extremely rewarding triumph.

To the words 'memorable' and 'extremely rewarding' perhaps we could add 'surprising'. It seems very strange to regard any Faldo victory as a surprise but the Englishman's 1994 season had hitherto been a very unsatisfactory one by his standards. Moreover, with double-Major winner (and defending champion) Nick Price and US Open winner Ernie Els in the starting line-up at Sun City, few imagined that the $1 million dollar first prize would be leaving the Southern Hemisphere.

As at Muirfield in '92, it was in the second round that Faldo established the platform for his success. Leading Els and Bernhard Langer by two after his opening 66, he went out in a steady 35 on Friday then birdied five successive holes from the 10th and added further birdies at the 16th and 17th to be home in 29: 'The

best nine holes of golf I have every played'. After that it should have been the proverbial cakewalk – but it wasn't. Just as he did at Muirfield, Faldo contrived to make it interesting. Ernie Els played his part too.

In front of his vociferous home fans, the South African fired a 67 in the third round then, as Faldo faltered, he rolled in a 30 footer for a birdie putt on the 4th hole on Sunday to tie for the lead. Faldo didn't have to play 'the best four holes of my life' to win (nor the best 14) but he finished more like the Nick Faldo of 1992 than the 1994 vintage and on the back nine it was Els who fell away, eventually allowing Price to claim second place. This time there was no rendition of 'My Way' at the prize giving ceremony; instead Faldo turned to the vast, expectant crowd and said, 'Sun City, thanks a million!' Hollywood beckons.

(Above) Ernie Els threatened to catch Nick Faldo on Sunday. (Below) Shades of Muirfield at Sun City

REST OF THE WORLD

GOLF IN ASIA

I t may have become something of a golfers' cliché but the game in Asia is genuinely booming. The Asian Tour, which has traditionally run from the beginning of February until the end of April and in 1994 comprised ten tournaments, will boast between sixteen and eighteen dates in 1995. A series of events will be staged in September and October with total prize money scheduled to increase from approximately $4 million to $7 million.

The Asian Tour is perhaps the most truly international circuit of all the world's tours. A glance at the list of tournament winners from 1994 reveals that golfers from seven different continents triumphed. There were two 'firsts' last year when Carlos Franco became the first Paraguayan to win on the Tour, when he won the Philippine Open and 20 year old Taiwanese golfer, Hong Chia-yu became the first amateur to win the Republic of China Open. The 1994 season was in fact one of the most exciting for years with half of the tournaments being decided by sudden death play-offs (it took Sweden's Joakim Haeggman eight extra holes before he claimed the Malaysian Open!) Among the big name winners on the Tour were Jumbo Ozaki, who collected his fourth 'White Jacket' at the Dunlop International Open and David Frost who won the Hong Kong Open.

In addition to hosting tournaments 'for the world' so other tours have chosen to stage events in Asia. Global sponsors (attracted in part, no doubt, by the variety of exotic locations) have realised the region's growth potential. Last year Greg Norman captured the PGA European Tour's Johnnie Walker Classic in Thailand and Jack Kay won the Alfred Dunhill Asian Masters, an Australasian Tour event, after Nick Faldo was sensationally disqualified on the final day.

Final proof of the 'boom' – if any were needed – will come in November 1995 with the playing of the 41st Heineken World Cup in Shenzhen, China.

Leading Chinese golfer, Zhen Wen-jun

1994 ASIAN TOUR

TOURNAMENT WINNERS

Philippine Open	Carlos Franco
Hong Kong Open	David Frost
Indian Open	Emlyn Aubrey
Thailand Open	Brandt Jobe
Malaysian Open	Joakim Haeggman
Indonesian Open	Frank Nobilo
Sabah Masters	Craig McClellan
Republic of China Open	Hong Chia-Yuh
Korean Open	Kim Jong-Duck
Dunlop International Open	Masashi Ozaki

Masashi Ozaki won the 1994 Dunlop International Open

NEWSWEEK ORDER OF MERIT

1	Carlos Franco	827
2	Brandt Jobe	708
3	Jim Rutledge	686
4	Lee Porter	683
5	Emlyn Aubrey	663
6	Mike Tschetter	617
7	Jerry Smith	577
8	Steve Flesch	512
9	Philip Jonas	494
10	Don Walsworth	491

February 3 - 6

JOHNNIE WALKER CLASSIC

BLUE CANYON CC, PHUKET, THAILAND

Greg Norman	75	70	64	68	277	£100000
Fred Couples	66	72	70	70	278	66660
Bernhard Langer	68	70	71	70	279	37560
Ian Woosnam	68	72	68	73	281	30000
Mike Harwood	71	72	69	70	282	25400
Colin Montgomerie	70	72	71	70	283	19500
Chin-Sheng Hsieh	70	69	70	74	283	19500
Frankie Minoza	72	74	67	71	284	14220
David Feherty	69	71	73	71	284	14220
Pierre Fulke	74	70	72	69	285	11106
Isao Aoki	70	71	71	73	285	11106
Sven Struver	77	70	69	69	285	11106

November 3 - 6

ALFRED DUNHILL ASIAN MASTERS

BALI GOLF & COUNTRY CLUB, NUSA DUA, BALI

J Kay	73	66	66	72	277	Aus$83,918
P Burke	68	70	70	70	278	47,554
V Singh	75	70	67	67	279	31,469
C Montgomerie	68	75	71	66	280	19,270
T Price	71	73	68	68	280	19,270
C Parry	70	67	71	72	280	19,270
N Van Rensburg	69	73	70	69	281	13,675
M Campbell	71	70	69	71	281	13,675
D Frost	70	70	70	71	281	13,675
M Cunning	67	74	71	70	282	10,956
N Faldo	67	63	69	disq		

Canada's Jack Kay was the winner in Bali

1994 GENE SARAZEN WORLD OPEN

During an interview last August, 92 year old Gene Sarazen was asked to name his favourite golf course, the finest player he had ever seen and the golfer he thought had the greatest potential to become a legend. His answers were: Augusta National, Jack Nicklaus and Ernie Els.

Three months later at a golf course called 'The Legends at Chateau Elan', situated no great distance from Augusta in Braselton, Georgia – indeed with a clubhouse and a number of holes directly modelled on Augusta – he watched Ernie Els win the inaugural Gene Sarazen World Open Championship. He saw him win it with a final day display that, not only bore an uncanny resemblance to Jack Nicklaus' finest hour in the Masters, but which included an approach shot to a par five hole that reminded everyone of Sarazen's famous 'Shot Heard Round the World' – the double-eagle of '35. It sounds improbable doesn't it? But it happened.

Little-known Fred Funk, who had qualified for this first gathering of 'the world's national Open champions' by winning the Mexican Open, looked set for a surprise victory as the final round unravelled. Funk held a two shot lead after three rounds and was five strokes ahead of Els after eight holes on Sunday.

...Five back with 10 to play, remember Augusta, 1986? Then, Nicklaus birdied the 9th and stormed the back nine in 30 strokes for a round of 65 to win his sixth Green Jacket.

Last November Els birdied the 9th on Sunday and charged home in 30 for a round of 65 to claim an extraordinary triumph. He birdied the 10th, 13th, 15th and 16th holes and he eagled the par five 14th, almost holing his second shot for a two. 'That was the most exciting tournament in my lifetime', said a stunned and delighted Sarazen.

Only in Georgia, it seems, are dreams lived, miracles delivered and legends born.

A legend and a future legend? Gene Sarazen presents the trophy to Ernie Els

November 3 - 6

GENE SARAZEN WORLD OPEN CHAMPIONSHIP

THE LEGENDS AT CHATEAU ELAN, BRASELTON, GEORGIA

E Els	67	73	68	65	273	$350,000
F Funk	69	69	66	72	276	200,000
M Calcavecchia	69	73	68	70	280	106,400
T Sieckmann	67	69	71	73	280	106,400
E Romero	69	73	71	68	281	72,200
C Rocca	73	72	67	70	282	56,525
M Roe	69	72	71	70	282	56,525
J Haeggman	72	70	69	71	282	56,525
M McNulty	71	67	73	71	282	56,525
M A Jimenez	72	66	68	77	283	45,600
G Turner	74	72	71	67	284	36,575
S Elkington	74	67	73	70	284	36,575
I Woosnam	72	71	72	69	284	36,575
J Parnevik	65	76	71	72	284	36,575

1994 JOHNNIE WALKER WORLD CHAMPIONSHIP

To become 'World Champion' is every sportsman's dream, but few sports afford the opportunity to achieve the honour in paradise. Golf, fortunately, is one such sport, and the beautiful Tryall Club, set against the dazzling blue Caribbean Sea on Jamaica's north-west coast, is the sublime

and Masters Champion José-Maria Olazabal were notable absentees, the elite 24-man field still positively oozed class. It contained eleven major winners, including all three previous World Champions, Messrs Couples, Faldo and Mize and, for the first time, Nick Price, the indisputable World Number One in 1994. The

Blue skies over Montego Bay: a perfect December day in Jamaica

setting for its annual 'crowning' ceremony.

So last December, for the fourth successive year, the world's finest golfers assembled near Montego Bay for the fitting finale to the season: the $2.5 million Johnnie Walker World Championship.

While World Number Two Greg Norman

hilly lay-out confronting them in the sweltering tropical heat possessed firm fairways and slick greens and with the sea-breezes always a crucial factor, claiming the $550,000 first prize would clearly require a good deal of hard work.

For Ernie Els, however, golf looks anything but hard work. The big-hitting South African

with the effortlessly, rhythmical swing and nonchalant smile makes the game look so ridiculously easy it is almost untrue. Last year, Ernie shot a first round 66 at Tryall for a one stroke lead; this year, it was a brilliant 64 (seven under par) containing a remarkable eight birdies in the last 10 holes, for a three stroke lead, but, whereas in 1993 he fell away to finish joint 8th, this time he remained in command with a vengeance.

Ernie Els spread-eagled the field with opening rounds of 64-64. Seve Ballesteros congratulates Paul Azinger on his record-equalling 62

By the time a second consecutive 64 (a score equalled by David Gilford on Friday) had given him a record 128 (14 under par) halfway score and a six stroke lead, Els had assumed complete control. The only hope for his pursuers seemed the unlikely prospect that he might self-destruct.

For a while during the third round this appeared possible but he recovered from a shaky start to record a level par 71 and finished the day seven strokes ahead of Nick Price. Had his nearest rivals, Nick Faldo (67-67) and Tom Lehman (69-65) maintained form it could have been a different story, but both met with disaster on the back nine (Faldo finding a watery grave at the short 13th and Lehman twice driving out of bounds) and rounds of 73 and 75, respectively, effectively ended their

**Nick Faldo, the champion in 1992
finished joint second behind Els**

December 15-18
JOHNNIE WALKER WORLD CHAMPIONSHIP
TRYALL, MONTEGO BAY, JAMAICA

Ernie Els	64	64	71	69	268	$550,000
Nick Faldo	67	67	73	67	274	250,000
Mark McCumber	67	70	70	67	274	250,000
Brad Faxon	72	70	69	64	275	106,666
Paul Azinger	71	74	62	68	275	106,666
Ian Woosnam	70	68	69	68	275	106,666
David Gilford	71	64	73	68	276	80,000
Jeff Maggert	68	72	70	66	276	80,000
Bernhard Langer	70	70	68	68	276	80,000
Robert Allenby	69	71	69	68	277	68,000
Colin Montgomerie	67	74	67	69	277	68,000
Nick Price	71	67	68	72	278	63,500
Tom Lehman	69	65	75	69	278	63,500
David Frost	70	71	74	68	283	61,500
Seve Ballesteros	73	72	65	73	283	61,500
Tom Kite	71	73	68	73	285	60,000
John Huston	73	73	70	70	286	57,500
Craig Parry	72	71	69	74	286	57,500
Loren Roberts	68	71	76	71	286	57,500
Fred Couples	73	65	75	73	286	57,500

championship hopes.

Though Tom Kite celebrated a hole in one at the 13th, it was golf itself which had most cause to celebrate on Saturday at Tryall. America's Paul Azinger, in the company of arch Ryder Cup foe Seve Ballesteros, produced a sensational course record 62 – the most heart-warming round of the year and confirmation that the courageous former USPGA champion is well on the road to recovery following his intensive lymphoma treatment. Ballesteros, incidentally, scored a 65.

Big Ernie completed his stroll in paradise on Sunday with a rock solid 69, for a comfortable six stroke victory over Nick Faldo and Mark McCumber. With a final day best 64 (which included a back nine of 30), Brad Faxon finished joint fourth alongside Azinger and Woosnam. Els' 268 (16 under par) aggregate was just two strokes behind Larry Mize's record 1993 score.

Victory over the old sugar plantation, his fifth success in 1994, certainly left a sweet taste in Ernie's mouth, for it completed a unique treble of world titles (Matchplay, Open and Championship) – all in a year's work for the 25 year old US Open champion.

By Richard Dyson

1994 AMATEUR GOLF REVIEW

Young, gifted and black; with the golfing world at his feet

Steel of the century: 18 year old Tiger Woods on his way to winning the 1994 US Amateur Championship

The burden of expectation is enormous: after the Bear came the Shark and after the Shark comes the Tiger. The future for Eldrick 'Tiger' Woods was mapped out long ago, and that is a truism whether one believes in destiny or not.

He was playing golf before he could walk. He was playing golf on television before he was five years old. Woods had won the United States Junior Championship by the time he was 15. He won it again when he was 16 and again when he was 17. Nobody had ever successfully defended that championship before. And no one had won the 'adult's version', the United States Amateur Championship before their 19th birthday − not even the Bear.

Jack Nicklaus was aged 19 years and eight months when he announced his arrival on the world stage by winning the 1959 US Amateur; last summer Tiger Woods was aged 18 years and seven months when he won the 1994 US Amateur. Not only was he the youngest ever champion but to achieve his victory he needed to effect the greatest ever comeback in the 94 year history of the championship. After 13 holes of his 36-hole final with Trip Kuehne he was six down − not the result of any wayward play on his part but because Kuehne had played superbly, scoring seven birdies. Woods was four down at the end of the morning round and still four down with eight holes to play... yet he managed to win on the final green.

Woods hails from Cypress, California; he is the son of a black father and a Thai mother and the golfing world is desperately interested to see how he performs at Augusta in April, the invitation coming courtesy of his victory over Kuehne.

Anyone doubting the extent of his reputation should have attended the World Amateur Team Championships at La Boulie, near Paris last September. His American team mates, all formidable players in their own right and more than capable of winning the biennial tournament with or without Woods, were happy to admit that the young prodigy had the ability to play golf to a standard that they could never hope to emulate.

Of course, many aspiring superstars have failed to fulfil their potential, thus we shall have to wait to discover if Tiger Woods really is 'the next Nicklaus'. One thing is certain: if he is only half as good as some are predicting, then Ernie Els and Phil Mickelson had better watch out.

While such headlines as 'Tiger, Tiger, Burning Bright' were being splashed across the sports pages of America last summer, British amateur golf enthusiasts were having to cope with, 'David slays Goliath' following the final of the British Amateur Championship at Nairn in Scotland. It was difficult to resist, mind you, not because any major upset had taken place but because a five foot seven inch golfer (England's Lee James) defeated a six foot eight inch player (Scotland's Gordon Sherry).

A second Englishman triumphed in a major national championship last year when Warren Bennett captured the Centenary Australian Amateur Championship at Royal Sydney in March. Bennett defeated the defending champion Greg Chalmers in the semi-final (Chalmers, incidentally, finished tied for eleventh in the Australian Open in November) then beat Victoria's Jamie McCallum in the

final. It was the start of an excellent year for Bennett who went on to win several important amateur titles in Europe and received the Silver Medal for finishing Leading Amateur in the British Open at Turnberry. We had also better mention that a Scottish golfer won the 1994 European Amateur Championship: Stephen Gallacher, the nephew of Europe's Ryder Cup captain, who claimed his title in Finland.

The major women's amateur event of 1994

Great Britain's Julie Hall and Lisa Walton study a putt during the 28th Curtis Cup match in Chattanooga

was the Curtis Cup match, held at the end of July at the Honors Course near Chattanooga. It was a thrilling contest, played in a marvellous spirit and, in the best traditions of recent transatlantic team encounters, its outcome remained uncertain until the final green of the final singles. The Curtis Cup is reviewed separately later in this chapter.

On the individual front, the Women's British Amateur Championship at Newport saw England's 22 year old Emma Duggleby defeat the experienced French player, Cecilia Morgue D'Algue by 3 & 1. Neither player was expected to reach the final; the match most 'connoisseurs' wanted to see, namely Julie Hall versus Catriona Matthew, took place in the

US Teams were successful in both the Men's and Women's
World Amateur Team Championships in Paris.
Wendy Ward (right) won the 1994
US Women's Amateur Championship

quarter-finals, with Matthew winning by 2 & 1.

The final of the US Women's Amateur Championship was contested by the 1993 champion, Jill McGill from Colorado and Wendy Ward from Texas, a semi-finalist in '93. Ward won impressively, by 2 & 1 and went on to play a starring role in the Women's World

Amateur Team Championships at La Boulie, eight days before Tiger Woods took Paris by storm in the men's event.

Actually, Woods didn't finish as Leading Individual at La Boulie – that award went to his team mate, 46 year old Allen Doyle and although Ward did secure individual honours, it was a 17 year old Korean, Se Ri Pak who captivated the galleries with a course record 65 on the final day.

1994 US AND BRITISH AMATEUR CHAMPIONSHIPS

August 22 - 28
US AMATEUR CHAMPIONSHIP
TPC AT SAWGRASS, PONTE VEDRA, FLORIDA

Quarter-Finals
T Woods beat T Jackson 5 & 4
T Kuehne beat C Raynor 2 up
K Cox beat E Gibstein 1 up
E Frishette beat J Curley 5 & 4
Semi-Finals
T Woods beat E Frishette 5 & 3
T Kuehne beat K Cox 1 up
Final
T Woods beat T Kuehne 2 up

May 30 - June 4
BRITISH AMATEUR CHAMPIONSHIP
NAIRN, LOTHIAN, SCOTLAND

Quarter-Finals
L James beat D Watson 5 & 4
G Sherry beat R Shiels 2 & 1
K Brink beat C Duke at 19th
A Turnbull beat M Erlandsson at 19th
Semi-Finals
L James beat A Turnbull 2 & 1
C Sherry beat K Brink 4 & 3
Final
L James beat G Sherry 2 & 1

Lee James,
the 1994
British Amateur
champion

August 8 - 14
US WOMEN'S AMATEUR CHAMPIONSHIP
THE HOMESTEAD (CASCADES), HOT SPRINGS, VIRGINIA

Quarter-Finals
W Ward beat R Higashio 7 & 5
J McGill beat J Erdmann 5 & 4
E Klein beat P Pedersen at 19th
A Baxter beat K Booth 2 & 1
Semi-Finals
W Ward beat A Baxter 7 & 5
J McGill beat E Klein 1 hole
Final
W Ward beat J McGill 2 & 1

June 7 - 11
BRITISH WOMEN'S AMATEUR CHAMPIONSHIP
NEWPORT, GWENT, WALES

Quarter-Finals
E Duggleby beat K Stupples at 19th
C Morgue D'Algue beat K Egford 2 & 1
C Matthew beat J Hall 2 & 1
A-J Adamson beat M Alsuguren 2 holes
Semi-Finals
E Duggleby beat A-J Adamson 2 & 1
C Morgue D'Algue beat C Matthew at 20th
Final
E Duggleby beat C Morgue D'Algue 3 & 1

THE 1994 CURTIS CUP

The 28th Curtis Cup always promised to be a close encounter and my goodness how it lived up to expectations! For the second time running, the event went the full distance and frayed the nerves of even the most hardened individual. Staged for the first time in the American South, Liz Boatman's young team travelled to steamy Chattanooga with high hopes of retaining the trophy, won in such dramatic fashion two years earlier at Hoylake. On paper, there seemed little to choose between Great Britain and Ireland and Lancy Smith's Americans. The home side were a couple or so years older on average, but each team included just two players with previous Cup experience. But, whereas Welsh stalwart Vicky Thomas had been surprisingly excluded, 45 year-old Carol Semple Thompson was in for a US record-equalling eighth appearance.

A half-hour delay, caused by mist, heightened the tension for the opening morning's play. Both captains fielded their strongest player in the crucial top match and when Julie Hall, playing her fourth Cup in a row, halved with US Amateur Champion Jill McGill the pattern for the contest was set.

The home side began better and the visitors were relieved to go to lunch trailing just 3½ – 2½, after six tight singles. The day seemed destined to end all-square, when after one emphatic afternoon foursomes win apiece, Scots Catriona Matthew and Janice Moodie looked set to go dormie three up over Jill McGill and Sarah LeBrun Ingram. However, the US pair saved, indeed nearly won the hole after receiving a fortuitous drop on the green when injury-hampered LeBrun Ingram's approach to

the par four 15th found the lake. The decision, though correct, caused controversy – exacerbated when the Americans went on to halve the match and finish the day 5-4 ahead.

GB & Ireland were far from despondent, however, and battled back to claim the final morning's foursomes 2-1, to level the match at 6-6 and set up a decisive afternoon singles series. An hour's thunderstorm break delayed the drama but on resumption America forged ahead. With McGill, Ellen Port and Wendy Ward all on their way to comfortable wins, the visitors' hopes rested on a trio of young Scots. They did not disappoint. Matthew (the event's only unbeaten player) handed 19 year old

Scottish heroines, Catriona Matthew and Janice Moodie

Emilee Klein her first setback and when Myra McKinlay followed suit the tension was mounting, as all eyes turned to the final match.

Trailing 9-8, outright victory was beyond GB & Ireland, but if Moodie (all-square with three to play) could force a win from her match, the Cup would be retained. The problem, though, was that her opponent was the 'veteran' Semple Thompson, winner of all three of her matches so far: surely her vast experience would tell? What followed was the most joyous flowering of youth, as, actually revelling under the pressure and showing maturity beyond her years, 21 year old Moodie claimed the 16th, halved the 17th and then clinched victory on the final hole in the most imperious manner. Her 165 yards, 6-iron approach to within five feet at the 18th will live long in the memory. So it was 'honours even' at The Honors Course, and GB & Ireland paraded the trophy for the fourth time in the last five meetings.

Killarney awaits a close encounter of the third kind in 1996.

July 30-31
28TH CURTIS CUP
THE HONORS COURSE, CHATTANOOGA, TENNESSEE

DAY ONE

Singles

J McGill halved with J Hall

E Klein bt J Moodie 3 & 2

W Ward lost to L Walton 1 hole

C Semple Thompson bt M McKinley 2 & 1

E Port bt M McKay 2 & 1

S Sparks lost C Matthew 1 hole

USA 3½ GB & Ireland 2½

Foursomes

J McGill & S LeBrun Ingram halved with C Matthew & J Moodie

C Semple Thompson & E Klein bt M McKay & K Speak 7 & 5

W Kaupp & E Port lost to J Hall & L Walton 6 & 5

USA 1½ GB & Ireland 1½

DAY TWO

Foursomes

J McGill & S LeBrun Ingram lost to J Hall & L Walton 2 & 1

C Semple Thompson & E Klein bt M McKinlay & E R Power 4 & 2

W Ward & S Sparks lost to C Matthew & J Moodie 3 & 2

USA 1 GB & Ireland 2

Singles

J McGill bt J Hall 4 & 3

E Klein lost to C Matthew 2 & 1

E Port bt M McKay 7 & 5

W Kaupp lost to M McKinlay 3 & 2

W Ward bt L Walton 4 & 3

C Semple Thompson lost to J Moodie 2 holes

USA 3 GB & Ireland 3

Match Result USA 9 GB & Ireland 9

Nine points they needed and nine points they got. Great Britain and Ireland retain the Curtis Cup

1994 SENIOR GOLF REVIEW

The story of Super Mex and the six million dollar men

'V' is for victory; Lee Trevino won six times on the US Senior Tour in 1994

It is generally accepted in America that there are far more 'personalities' playing the US Senior Tour than the regular PGA Tour. 'The fat bellies have more fun', according to Lee Trevino, and he should know. Every year, it seems, 'Super Mex' wins a hat full of tournaments and transports a million dollars to the bank; 1994 was no exception. He won six events on the Senior Tour, all before the end of July, after which he was hampered by a neck injury (not that this stopped him from smiling).

His winnings for the season totalled over $1.2 million. This was 'only' good enough for fourth place on the Money List, although it is reasonable to assume that had he not suffered the injury he would have ended the year in first position – with winnings in excess of those achieved by Nick Price on the PGA Tour.

With Trevino either side-lined or unable to produce his best golf, the jam was spread more evenly throughout the second half of 1994. Indeed no fewer than six players won more than a million dollars in prize money.

The Tour's four Majors were shared by four of its top stars – and four of its greatest personalities. Ray Floyd defeated Dale Douglass in a play-off to win The Tradition at Desert Mountain at the beginning of April; two weeks later Trevino made the most of an uncharacteristic collapse by Floyd to capture the USPGA Seniors' Championship at PGA National; Dave Stockton was a runaway winner of the Senior Players Championship over the TPC of Michigan in June and Simon Hobday held on to win the US Senior Open at Pinehurst.

The most memorable of the Majors, perhaps not surprisingly, given its magnificent venue, was the US Senior Open, the biggest prize in senior golf.

We mentioned the prevalence of 'personalities' on the Tour, well, they don't come more legendary than Simon Hobday, once described as the 'Oliver Reed of golf'. Hobday led for most of the week at Pinehurst but after brilliant rounds of 66-67-66 he stuttered (or should that be staggered) in sight of the finishing post. Chased by Jim Albus and an inspired Graham Marsh, he nearly lost the championship over the closing stretch before holing a knee-trembling two footer on the 18th green for victory – whereupon he collapsed in a heap. It was an altogether more rivetting and emotional conclusion than Ernie Els' triumph in the US Open at Oakmont. It also confirmed that the summer belonged to golfers from Southern Africa.

Among other noteworthy performances on the 1994 US Senior Tour was the extraordinary debut win by former 'Career-amateur' Jay Sigel.

Playing in only his fourth professional tournament, he came from 10 strokes behind on the final day to win the GTE West Classic with an eight under par 62. Sigel almost repeated the feat in the season-ending Tour Championship (won by Floyd after a dramatic play-off) when he fired a closing 63 which

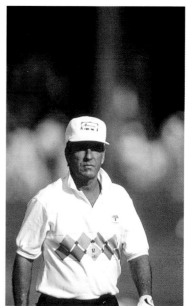

Winners and personalities: (top left) Isao Aoki; (top right) Simon Hobday at the US Senior Open; (left) Dave Stockton, the Tour's Leading Moneywinner in 1994

included an amazing double-eagle on the back nine. Not a bad way to finish a first season in senior golf!

Another player who appears to have adapted well to life on the Tour is Japan's Isao Aoki who recorded back-to-back victories late in the

American Tom Wargo captured the British Senior Open title at Royal Lytham. (Far left) Gary Player finished in a tie for fourth

season. After his seven wins on the Japanese PGA Tour last year, forty-seven year old Jumbo Ozaki must surely be licking his lips in anticipation.

Britain's Tony Jacklin turned fifty in June 1994. Anxious to renew acquaintances (and perhaps settle a few old scores with the likes of Lee Trevino) he enrolled on the US Senior Tour and before the end of the season had mounted the winner's rostrum.

His much-awaited debut in Europe took place at the Senior British Open at Royal Lytham and St Annes, the scene of his famous triumph in the 1969 Open Championship. Unfortunately the hero's welcome turned sour when he was disqualified after he signed for an incorrect score on the opening day. It was a fine championship, nonetheless: Arnold Palmer rolled back the years to lead after the first round with a 69 – despite being three over par for his first five holes; defending champion Bob Charles put up a stirring defence, but it was American Tom Wargo who eventually made off with the trophy.

Oh, yes, and Gary Player gave a superb demonstration in the art of bunker play.

1994 SENIOR MAJORS

28 March - 3 April
THE TRADITION
DESERT MOUNTAIN, SCOTTSDALE, ARIZONA

R Floyd	65	70	68	68	271	$127,500
D Douglass	68	68	69	66	271	74,800
(Floyd won play-off at first extra hole)						
J Colbert	70	66	68	70	274	61,200
J Nicklaus	70	71	69	68	278	41,933
J Powell	67	69	72	70	278	41,933
T Weiskopf	68	70	70	70	278	41,933
G Gilbert	66	69	73	71	279	28,900
M Hill	70	70	68	71	279	28,900
I Aoki	67	69	71	73	280	22,100

11 - 17 April
USPGA SENIORS' CHAMPIONSHIP
PGA NATIONAL, PALM BEACH GARDENS, FLORIDA

L Trevino	70	69	70	70	279	$115,000
J Colbert	68	71	74	67	280	85,000
R Floyd	69	69	69	75	282	57,500
D Stockton	70	69	71	72	282	57,500
I Aoki	71	71	75	66	283	32,500
D Weaver	72	73	70	68	283	32,500
D Douglass	70	71	70	72	283	32,500
C C Rodriguez	73	72	69	69	283	32,500
J Nicklaus	71	71	72	72	286	20,500

22 - 26 June
FORD SENIOR PLAYERS CHAMPIONSHIP
TPC OF MICHIGAN, DEARBORN, MICHIGAN

D Stockton	66	66	71	68	271	$210,000
J Albus	67	69	72	69	277	123,200
I Aoki	67	70	73	68	278	84,000
R Floyd	72	68	71	67	278	84,000
L Trevino	66	69	74	69	278	84,000
J Nicklaus	68	72	73	67	280	50,400
H Henning	69	67	74	70	280	50,400
J Dent	72	67	70	71	280	50,400
J Sigel	67	71	73	70	281	39,200

30 June - 3 July
US SENIOR OPEN
PINEHURST NO.2, NORTH CAROLINA

S Hobday	66	67	66	75	274	$145,000
J Albus	66	69	66	74	275	63,418
G Marsh	68	68	69	70	275	63,418
T Weiskopf	72	66	72	67	277	30,608
T Wargo	69	70	68	70	277	30,608
D Stockton	74	67	68	68	277	30,608
B Murphy	71	70	71	67	279	21,651
J Sigel	73	66	70	70	279	21,651
J Nicklaus	69	68	70	72	279	21,651
I Aoki	69	71	73	67	280	18,313
L Trevino	69	71	72	69	281	17,169
R Floyd	69	68	74	71	282	16,044
D Eichelberger	74	72	69	69	284	14,280
G Player	72	67	73	72	284	14,280
R Thompson	70	74	69	71	284	14,280

US SENIOR TOUR MONEY LIST

1	Dave Stockton	$1,402,519
2	Ray Floyd	1,382,762
3	Jim Albus	1,237,128
4	Lee Trevino	1,202,369
5	Jim Colbert	1,012,115
6	Tom Wargo	1,005,344
7	Jim Dent	950,891
8	Bob Murphy	855,862
9	Larry Gilbert	848,544
10	George Archer	717,578

20 - 23 July
SENIOR BRITISH OPEN CHAMPIONSHIP
ROYAL LYTHAM AND ST ANNES, LANCASHIRE

T Wargo	73	68	68	71	280	£36,650
B Charles	70	69	72	71	282	18,905
D Dalziel	75	66	71	70	282	18,905
G Player	73	69	71	74	287	10,165
B Huggett	78	68	70	71	287	10,165
J Morgan	71	73	71	73	288	7,150
A Palmer	69	74	71	74	288	7,150
T Horton	71	72	71	75	289	5,500

1995
A Year to Savour

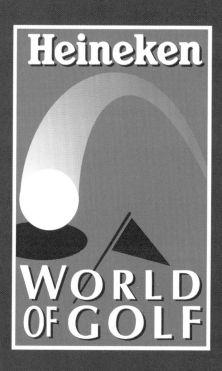

1995 MAJORS

A Preview by Richard Dyson

A year that can boast the Centenary US Open at revered Shinnecock Hills and a record 25th Open Championship at St Andrews, the Home of Golf itself, is bound to be eagerly anticipated. As the oldest venues on the current Open rotas of the USGA and R & A respectively, the champions these two great courses produce will truly be following in historic footsteps. With the major line-up completed by the perennial highlight of the Masters at Augusta National and the USPGA at Riviera – that playground of the rich and famous – 1995 promises to be a mouth-watering prospect indeed.

Particular attention this year is bound to be paid, collectively, to the exploits of American golfers and specifically, to the performances of a certain Zimbabwean by the name of Nicholas Raymond Leige Price. While the latter positively sizzled in 1994 with Open/USPGA success, the former resembled the proverbial damp squib in finishing a full Grand Slam campaign without a winner in their midst for the first time.

As the US desperately searches for its first superstar since Tom Watson, Price is clearly the major man of the moment. In becoming the first player to win successive majors since Watson's transatlantic Open double of 1982 (ironically a result of Price's collapse at Royal Troon) and the first to win two in the same

Nick Price, the 'major man of the moment'

The 19th hole
at Augusta
National

year since fellow David Leadbetter protégé Nick Faldo in 1990, this genial champion now has three Grand Slam victories to his name.

Price's chance to equal Ben Hogan's feat of claiming three different majors consecutively will come at Augusta in April where he will be strongly fancied for the 59th Masters. A first Green Jacket surely awaits if he can reproduce the form of his course record 63, set in 1986. However, any speculation as to who may become the 1995 'Master' golfer simply can't

ignore the remarkable recent European factor. Last year José-Maria Olazabal became the sixth European winner in the last seven years and with nine winners in the last 15 years, since Seve opened the floodgates in 1980, one could be forgiven for thinking that the 'European' Masters is staged annually in Georgia and not at Crans-sur-Sierre!

The three other foreign wins in the Masters all belong to Gary Player. Now, in Ernie Els (prominent last year until the 13th proved to

Amen for Ernie: the 1994 US Open champion came to grief at Augusta's fabled 13th in last year's Masters. Will 1995 be his year?

be his unlucky hole in the final round), South Africa undoubtedly has another potential champion. The burden of home expectation may fall upon the broad shoulders of Tom Lehman: joint 3rd ('93), 2nd ('94), 1st (95)? Much too will be expected of Fred Couples, the last US winner, an absentee through injury from 1994's event.

It's become a cliché but true nonetheless – the Masters doesn't really begin until the back

recall the most famous of them all. 1995 marks the 60th Anniversary of Gene Sarazen's 4 wood double eagle – 'the shot heard around the world' and undeniably the making of the Masters.

Come June there will be an even more significant anniversary to celebrate, namely, the Centenary US Open Championship (though, because of World Wars, actually only the 95th). What strides have been made since the

Colin Montgomerie's game should be ideally suited to Shinnecock Hills, venue for the Centenary US Open

nine on Sunday afternoon. Each hole is beautiful, each is beguiling and in the last two years it's been the 500 yards, par five, 15th which has been decisive. Over the years, many great shots have been executed amidst Augusta's azaleas, dogwoods and pines, but competitors striding over Sarazen Bridge to the 15th green this year will have special reason to

first official US Open was contested, by just 11 players, over four rounds of the nine hole course at Newport Golf Club, Rhode Island on October 4, 1895! Englishman Horace Rawlins' first prize then was $150, seemingly insignificant when compared with Ernie Els' $320,000 reward last year, yet one thing has never changed and that is the priceless honour

**The 13th hole
at Shinnecock
Hills**

of being hailed as National Open Champion of America.

The Centenary US Open will be staged at historic Shinnecock Hills Golf Club on Long Island, New York. This highly exclusive club near the fashionable summer resort of Southampton, has played a key pioneering role in American golf. It was at Shinnecock that Scotsman James Foulis won the 2nd US Open in 1896 and, where 90 years later Raymond Floyd, thanks to a closing 66, became the oldest ever US Open champion.

After Foulis and Floyd maybe Faldo will complete a hat-trick of winners sharing the same surname initial? He will no doubt take heart from the fact the Shinnecock is widely considered to be the American course most reminiscent of a British links. However, after two near misses in the last three years, Colin Montgomerie must be regarded as Europe's leading hope. Accurate driving, Monty's great strength, is at a premium at Shinnecock, where tight fairways and deep rough allied to constant and variable coastal winds offer no respite for the wayward.

Overseas hopes will be high after home domination, stretching back to 1982, was ended last year at Oakmont where the USGA also provided a welcome and more generous foreign allocation. Greg Norman, for whom Shinnecock was part two of his 1986 'Saturday Slam', must be strongly fancied and the Australian may consider it a good omen that it was fellow countryman Kel Nagle who triumphed in the Centenary British Open.

Tom Watson, who had such an impressively consistent major campaign in 1994 could well lead the American challenge, certainly there would be no more popular Centenary US Open champion. However, for a suitably historic scenario to such a special occasion, perhaps Hale Irwin, a winner on the 1994 US PGA Tour and the man who succeeded Floyd as the event's oldest winner in 1990, could join that illustrious quartet of Anderson, Jones, Hogan and Nicklaus as a record four time US Open winner.

The Centenary Open Championship was held in 1960 when the aforementioned Nagle thwarted Arnold Palmer's Grand Slam hopes at St Andrews. This year it is to the Old Course that the 124th Open returns in July for a

Enter at your peril: the notorious Road Hole bunker on the 17th at St Andrews

record 25th time, surpassing the mark previously shared with Prestwick, where 70 years ago Jim Barnes won the last Open staged over the event's original venue.

The combination of the world's oldest championship with the Home of Golf provides an atmosphere unique in the sport. There are Opens and there are St Andrews Opens and as Jack Nicklaus once said, 'if you want to be remembered you have got to win at St Andrews'. The Golden Bear did, of course, win consecutive St Andrews Opens in the 1970s, emulating the feats of Triumvirate members, John H Taylor and James Braid at the turn of the century. The only other man to win two Opens in the auld grey toon, since Tom Kidd claimed the first there in 1873, being Scotsman Bob Martin.

St Andrews, means the Road Hole, the most famous and feared card wrecker in the game. This fiendish 461 yards, par 4, 17th is bound to play a key role in the outcome of the championship and in the 1990 Open yielded just 15 birdies during the entire event, when playing to an average of 4.65. This year's champion must, if not conquer the hole, then at least be able to limit the damage, for Seve in 1984 and Faldo in 1990 each managed just one par and three bogeys there en route to victory.

That 1990 Open triumph, achieved by a 5 stroke margin, saw Faldo at the peak of his powers. As defending champion over the course he will, along with the other famous Nick, defending champion Price, start as one of the favourites for the title.

No American has won the Open in the 1990s, but they can claim in Curtis Strange, the current course record holder at St Andrews, the double US Open winner having blitzed a 62 during the 1987 Dunhill Cup. The fact that this team event has been staged here for the last 10 years means that more players are now aware of the intricacies of this peerless links and could well result in a very tight Open.

Spectators at the Dunhill Cup have become accustomed to 'extra-time' drama, maybe this year will see the first Open play-off since 1989 – now that would be a prospect to savour!

Win a major championship and celebrity status follows, but the golfers won't be the only stars at Riviera Country Club in August for the 77th USPGA Championship. This famous Californian course is renowned for its show business members and is well known to the players as the host club of the Los Angeles Open on the PGA Tour. The luxuriantly beautiful George Thomas designed lay-out at Pacific Palisades plays long and represents a formidable test of golfing skills.

The 1995 USPGA will be the third major to be staged at Riviera. Ben Hogan won his first US Open here in 1948 with a record 276 aggregate which lasted for 19 years and in 1983 Hal Sutton held off a final round Nicklaus charge to claim the title with a score of 274.

Hogan, through his exploits in the LA Open (it was here in 1950 that he made his post car crash comeback) and the subsequent shooting of his film story 'Follow The Sun' at the club, is indelibly linked with Riviera.

Recently, however, the man to beat here has been big-hitting Fred Couples. Californian born Corey Pavin, another Riviera winner and runner-up in last year's USPGA should also figure strongly. This gritty competitor is overdue a major breakthrough and could go one better this time. With two wins in the last three years though, defending champion Nick Price is clearly the USPGA form man.

One thing is certain, Riviera's natural amphitheatre surrounding the 18th green and the imposing clubhouse looking down upon it will be packed with appreciative golf fans. A feast awaits them, as it does the galleries at Augusta, Shinnecock and St Andrews. Roll on the 1995 majors!

1995 Major Championship Dates

April 6 - 9	The Masters
June 15 - 18	The US Open
July 20 - 23	The Open Championship
Aug 10 - 13	The USPGA

The final hole of the final Major: the 18th at the Riviera Country Club, where Nick Price will defend his USPGA title in August

RYDER CUP HISTORY

UNITED STATES 23, GREAT BRITAIN/EUROPE 5, TIES 2

1927	Worcester CC, Worcester, Mass.	US 9½, Britain 2½
1929	Moortown, Yorkshire, England	Britain 7, US 5
1931	Scioto CC, Columbus, Ohio	US 9, Britain 3
1933	Southport & Ainsdale, England	Britain 6 ½, US 5½
1935	Ridgewood CC, Ridgewood, NJ	US 9, Britain 3
1937	Southport & Ainsdale, England	US 8, Britain 4
	Ryder Cup not contested during World War II	
1947	Portland Golf Club, Portland, Ore	US 11, Britain 1
1949	Ganton GC, Scarborough, England	US 7, Britain 5
1951	Pinehurst CC, Pinehurst, NC	US 9½, Britain 2½
1953	Wentworth, Surrey, England	US 6½, Britain 5½
1955	Thunderbird Ranch & CC, Palm Springs, Ca.	
		US 8, Britain 4
1957	Lindrick GC, Yorkshire, England	Britain 7½, US 4½
1959	Eldorado CC, Palm Desert, Ca.	US 8½, Britain 3½
1961	Royal Lytham & St Anne's GC, St Anne's-on-the-Sea, England	US 14½, Britain 9½
1963	East Lake CC, Atlanta, Ga.	US 23, Britain 9
1965	Royal Birkdale GC, Southport, England	
		US 19½, Britain 12½

1967	Champions GC, Houston, Tex.	US 23½, Britain 8½
1969	Royal Birkdale GC, Southport, England	
		US 16, Britain 16 (TIE)
1971	Old Warson CC, St Louis, Mo.	US 18½, Britain 13½
1973	Muirfield, Scotland	US 18, Britain 13
1975	Laurel Valley GC, Ligonier, Pa.	US 21, Britain 11
1977	Royal Lytham & St Anne's GC, St Anne's-on-the-Sea, England	US 12½, Britain 7½
1979	The Greenbrier, White Sulphur Springs, W. Va.	US 17, Europe 11
1981	Walton Heath GC, Surrey, England	US 18½, Europe 9½
1983	PGA National GC, Palm Beach Gdns, Fla.	US 14½ Europe 13½
1985	The Belfry, Sutton Coldfield, England	Europe 16½, US 11½
1987	Muirfield Village, Ohio	Europe 15, US 13
1989	The Belfry, Sutton Coldfield, England	Europe 14, US 14 (TIE)
1991	Kiawah Island, South Carolina	US 14½, Europe 13½
1993	The Belfry, Sutton Coldfield, England	US 15, Europe 13

1995 RYDER CUP

A Preview by David MacLaren

Reading the golfing press in 1994 could easily have led one to the conclusion that the 1995 Ryder Cup had, in fact, been cancelled, allowing everyone the opportunity of moving straight to the much lauded charms of Valderrama, 1997. The prospect of waiting until 1997 for the next Ryder Cup is, however, clearly an unthinkable one for those hordes of addicts on both sides of the Atlantic, for whom the biennial contest is even more important than the dollar nassau or 50p-a-quarter Sunday morning fourball.

Oak Hill in 1995, did someone say? Should that not be Oakmont, venue of so many memorable major championships? Or even Oakland Hills, the original 'monster' brought to its knees by Ben Hogan in 1951? No, Oak Hill is surely the sort of country club-style layout reserved for the mundane business of major championships; the Ryder Cup is pure showbusiness and only takes place on 8,000 yard monster layouts populated by khaki-clad alligators and tear-stained Scotsmen.

Ah, you say, surely the US PGA and the PGA European Tour can shed some light on the mystery of Oak Hill, 1995? Well, yes, a December call to the offices of both these esteemed bodies revealed that the next Ryder Cup will indeed be next held this year, and that the venue will be the East Course at Oak Hill. As to the make-up of the course: 'We hope to have a hole-by-hole guide sometime in the new year'. The players? 'Read the golf magazines'. A press release? 'Not since the announcement of Bernard Gallacher's re-appointment as Captain'.

Hardly encouraging. Perhaps it's all deliberate, a ploy to wrest the Ryder Cup back into the realms of a sporting event and away from the golfing equivalent of a bullfight. Just perhaps, someone has realised that the world will not actually self-destruct the morning after the closing ceremony – the Monday morning brigade will still skate round the local muni. in two and three-quarter hours and Nick Faldo will still be favourite for virtually every tournament he enters. And just perhaps, the powers-that-be have decided that the Ryder Cup, yes even the Ryder Cup, must be allowed to retain, or rather regain, its reputation for epitomising all that is pure and laudable in sport, rather than degenerating into yet another over-hyped pseudo sporting extravaganza, where real sporting values are obliterated by the needs of an avaricious media.

No-one can doubt of course that the last four stagings of the venerable old contest have in all probability saved Samuel Ryder's fragile gold trophy from a rapid descent into sporting oblivion. Without the efforts of all concerned to raise the temperature from that of a one-sided procession into three days of nerve-jangling, grip-twitching sporting theatre, it is doubtful whether the Ryder Cup would now be any more than one more end-of-season bonanza for our globetrotting superstars.

If The Belfry and Kiawah have revitalised one of sport's worthiest challenges, Oak Hill 1995 offers a not-to-be spurned opportunity of ensuring that sporting values largely peculiar to golf are once more given the chance to flourish. However distant the memories, it is never futile to revisit some of the moments that have shaped the reputation of the Ryder Cup, not only for moments of unequalled sporting

for the following two years, were dependent upon two putts of the distance that seems to provoke more terror in golfers' hearts than any other single shot. That Jack Nicklaus chose to concede to Tony Jacklin a putt of over two feet not only served to cement Nicklaus' reputation as a sportsman of the highest integrity but also established the Ryder Cup forever more as one of the few sporting contests not to have sold its soul to the evils of money and personal

Royal Lytham, 1961: The Ryder Cup as it was – note the vast crowds

tension but also as an opportunity for some of golf's finest exponents to show the regard with which they hold the traditions and values of the game.

Any worthwhile exposition of sporting values must make mention of the momentous struggle at Birkdale in 1969, when the respective personal reputations of Messrs Jacklin and Nicklaus, not to say the destiny of the Cup

egotism.

Moments of drama have peppered the history of the Ryder Cup, and not solely, as often imagined, since the introduction of players from continental Europe in order to redress what had become a very uneven contest. The West Course at Wentworth, to choose but one example, can include the 1953 Ryder Cup among its endless roll-call of golfing

drama. With two matches to go, the home team was ahead and was beaten to the post only through a series of heart-rending mishaps suffered by two of its most skilled young protagonists, Peter Alliss and Bernard Hunt. Consolation was relatively short in coming however, with the bulldog-type leadership of Dai Rees providing the basis for a memorable home victory four years later.

The hopes and fears provoked by such moments will doubtless not be far from the thoughts of twenty-four of the world's finest golfers when the flags are raised at this year's opening ceremony. Whilst it is doubtful whether tension equal to that experienced on the 18th green at Kiawah in 1991 will ever be repeated, Oak Hill 1995 will undoubtedly not fail to stir the entire spectrum of emotions in both players and spectators. New York State may seem an unlikely location for those seeking

(Above) The Belfry, 1989: frenzied scenes at the 18th as Europe retains the trophy. Dave Stockton (left) victor of the over-hyped 'War on the Shore' at Kiawah Island in 1991

to ensure that emotions provoked by sporting drama are kept in context; however Oak Hill is certainly one of those venerable American country club venues where the sheer pace of life would seem to preclude any danger of emotions surging out of control.

The East Course at Oak Hill, Rochester, New York was once described as being as close to perfection as any course in America. Any pilgrim reading this eulogy and expecting to

to find the signature of one Donald Ross on the layout at Oak Hill. Completed in 1926, the course betrays its creator with many of the archetypal Ross characteristics: raised and rolling greens, swales and valleys surrounding the putting surfaces, and the strategic positioning of bunkers designed to create confusion and uncertainty.

Although the principal feature of the course, unsurprisingly, is a collection of more than

The 1st at Oak Hill, venue for the 1995 Ryder Cup

find Augusta National, Pine Valley and Cypress Point all rolled into one is likely to be disappointed. However, whilst Oak Hill may never reach the peaks of other revered layouts, neither does it have any of the mundane or farcical holes that so often seem to blight otherwise world-class courses. Consistency of design is a quality sought after by all golf course architects and it comes as little surprise

thirty thousand oak trees of almost thirty varieties, Oak Hill sets out to impose its authority on the player from the outset. At 445 yards, the first hole is a narrow, unrelenting par four, with a customary creek providing an early grave for an underhit approach. It is possibly not until the back nine, however, that Oak Hill really bares its teeth, so much so that the 13th is often described as one of the best golf holes in the entire continent. The hole measures some 600 yards from the championship tee, with the aforementioned Allen Creek providing the golfing equivalent of a brick wall 300 yards distant. The second shot is played through the Hill of Fame; large stands of trees dedicated to heroes of golf and the state straddling both sides of an undulating fairway.

Oak Hill has one important characteristic in esque, or Kiawah-esque proportions. Turning sharply to the right at 260-270 yards around a cavernous bunker, the hole runs uphill towards a raised green that is jealously guarded by yet more sand. The precise unfolding of this year's contest can only be guessed at this stage; what is sure is that the nature of the golf course will do nothing but encourage the type of drama and emotion synonymous with Ryder Cups both distant and recent.

Oak Hill's 11th hole

common with all great Ryder Cup venues – a strong run of closing holes with the ability to change the course of a match – nay entire contest – within the scope of a few hundred yards. Holes 16, 17 and 18 are par fours in excess of 440 yards, all possessing both the length and severity to change the course of golfing history. The closing hole in particular, thankfully, has the potential to attain Belfry-

If the challenge posed by the venue can be stated with absolute certainty, the composition of the two teams is, at the onset of 1995, much more open to the sport of animated speculation which fills golf club bars on rainy Saturday afternoons. Doubtless, the months leading up to the contest will be accompanied by the usual feelings of terror on the European side of the Atlantic that all sorts of home 'bankers' are going to fall short of automatic selection. Memories will be recalled of the run-up to the 1993 contest, with an unseemly scramble both on the golf course and in the press in an attempt to ensure the inclusion of Europe's big guns. In retrospect, much momentum and adrenaline were used up in the run-up to the contest at The Belfry, leading to a number of jaded stars unable to reproduce the necessary sparkle.

Those armchair team captains who feel that the American selection process is more conducive to arriving at the right result would do well to reflect on the team standings at the end of 1994. A glance at the respective top fours in each list reads: Severiano Ballesteros, Bernhard Langer, José-Maria Olazabal and Ian Woosnam versus Loren Roberts, Corey Pavin, Tom Lehman and Fuzzy Zoeller.

What is certain is that many of the chief

Seve Ballesteros and José-Maria Olazabal at the 1989 Ryder Cup

actors in the unforgettable contests of the last twelve years will once more be present at Oak Hill, ensuring the resumption of many personal contests – 'vendettas' is not a word that need ever be mentioned in relation to golf – together with the usual influx of fresh talent from which a hero will inevitably emerge. The Ryder Cup is as much about the conquering of first-time nerves and the impudence of youth as it is about the gladiators of the game locking

the match with the imminent death of the game on the appropriate side of that water hazard known as the Atlantic. Such an excess of dramatisation should be avoided: the Ryder Cup does not change the face of golf, it only enhances it – a legacy that will surely be continued at Oak Hill in 1995.

Rising American star Phil Mickelson should make his Ryder Cup debut at Oak Hill

antlers in a battle of reputation and of will.

Oak Hill will provide a fitting stage for the unfolding of the latest chapter in the glorious and (latterly) unpredictable history of the Ryder Cup. When the dust has settled and the final putt holed – or missed – the result will matter far less than the fact that golf will once more be shown as the perfect medium for sports and sportsmanship to mingle in reasonably perfect harmony. Attempts will doubtless be made by both golfers and scribes to equate the loss of

1995 HEINEKEN WORLD OF GOLF

A Preview by Richard Dyson

Heineken's distinctive World of Golf logo has become a familiar sight in recent years and is now emblematic at some of the game's finest venues. Commencing with its own national championship in 1991, the famous Dutch brewer has associated itself with an international cross-section of prestigious golfing occasions, in a highly refreshing sponsorship initiative.

This year's four-event schedule once again promises great excitement, with the undoubted highlight being the opening up of a new golfing frontier with the historic staging of the Heineken World Cup in China. Completing Heineken's own 'Grand Slam' for 1995 will be

In early February, attention will focus on
The Vines Resort near Perth, Western Australia
as the club stages The Heineken Classic

the Heineken Dutch Open on the PGA European Tour, and, 'Down Under', the Heineken Classic and Heineken Australian Open, which respectively open and close the 1995 programme.

For the third year running, the Heineken Classic, in February, is an early year highlight on the Australasian Tour. Formerly known as The Vines Classic, its home is the idyllic Vines Resort, set amidst the vineyards of the Swan

Valley, close to Western Australia's vibrant capital city of Perth. In just a few years this event has already proved itself a great success, with fans in Australia's largest state showing their appreciation of the chance to see big-time golf – mostly the preserve of eastern centres such as Melbourne, Sydney and the Queensland coast.

The combination of excellent support, beautiful weather and a spectacular, modern, yet very natural lay-out, allied to magnificent resort facilities means that once again an impressive starting line-up is expected this year. Heineken are confident it will include 'Wild Thing' John Daly, who would be guaranteed to find parts of The Vines that others couldn't

possibly reach! The American crowd-pleaser should acquit himself rather better than last year's big name casualties, 1991 major champions, Ian Baker-Finch (winner here in 1992) and Ian Woosnam, who both missed the cut.

Defending champion will be Mike Clayton, who, in 1994, became the third consecutive home winner and second successive broom-handled putter (after Peter Senior in 1993) to claim the title. Clayton finished in style with a

Look out Perth! John Daly has agreed to play in the 1995 Heineken Classic

birdie on the demanding par five, 18th where water, prevalent on the back nine, must be avoided at all costs. His closing round of 70 for a 279 (nine under par) aggregate gave him a three stroke victory over fellow countryman Wayne Smith.

It's a tough task to follow the Open Championship, especially when it is at St Andrews, the Home of Golf, but it says much for the stature of the Heineken Dutch Open that many of the world's top golfers will assemble in the Netherlands, in late July, just a day or two after contesting the game's ultimate prize in the Kingdom of Fife. Like its British equivalent, the Dutch Open has a tradition of offering great seaside golf, with The Hague,

Noordwijkse and famed Kennemer representing continental links golf at its best.

However, for the second year in a row, the Heineken Dutch Open will be played inland in 1995, the venue, as last year, being delightful tree-lined Hilversum in Utrecht. A regular setting for the championship over the years, this esteemed club can boast a colourful list of past Dutch Open winners. Included amongst them are the event's record champions, Flory

aggregate of 270 to fend off a resurgent Howard Clark by 2 strokes. The man from Malaga admirably displayed the controlled aggression necessary for success at Hilversum, in claiming the biggest victory of his career. American Bob Byman (in 1978) was the last player to successfully defend the Dutch Open and Jimenez will have to overcome another world class field in his bid to retain one of the Volvo Tour's most popular and sought after

Miguel Angel Jimenez completes a Spanish victory in the 1994 Heineken Dutch Open at Hilversum
(Jiminez' reaction to holing the putt can be seen on page 98)

van Donck and famous Ryder Cup men, John Jacobs, Brian Huggett, Brian Barnes, Gordon Brand Jnr and of course, Seve Ballesteros.

Last year, another Spaniard (tipped by Seve for future Ryder Cup honours), namely, Miguel Angel Jimenez, was as 'hot' as the weather as he scorched round in a sizzling 18 under par

titles, now in its fifth year under the Heineken banner.

The brainchild of American industrialist John Jay Hopkins, the Canada Cup, as it was known when it was launched in that country in 1953, the World Cup as it became in 1967, has always been a special event which has captured the imagination, but rarely can it have been more eagerly anticipated than this year. In a bold and exciting venture it will break new ground this November when the hitherto golfing outpost of China, with its vast potential for the royal and ancient game, gets its first taste of top international action.

The world's most populous country may have been pipped for the Olympic Games in the year 2000, but in 1995 it will have the

Cup course, the beautiful short par five, 7th, where water is much in evidence, is reminiscent of the 13th at Augusta, while the short par four, 13th is another memorable hole. The venue also lays claim to possessing the largest and most comprehensive clubhouse facilities (to striking traditional design) in Asia.

Under Heineken's sponsorship, now in its third year, the World Cup is flourishing and for the second year running, two qualifiers: West

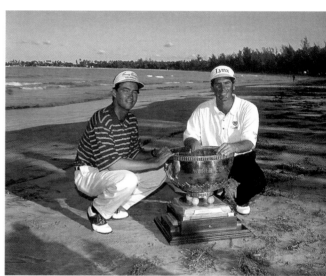

In July Hilversum (left) will again host the Heineken Dutch Open; it is not an especially difficult course... provided you keep to the fairways. From Spain to Florida to Puerto Rico to China: Fred Couples and Davis Love will be seeking their fourth successive victory at the 1995 Heineken World Cup in Shenzhen, China

honour of staging the 41st playing of the 'Olympics of Golf'. China will become the 29th host nation when 32 countries, each represented by two-man teams, gather at the Mission Hills Golf Club at Guan Lan Town, Shenzhen (near Hong Kong) in the south of the country.

This dramatic new development, nestling between rolling hills and framed by natural lakes boasts two championship courses designed to the exacting specifications of the event's most successful competitor himself, one Jack William Nicklaus. On the Heineken World

Zone (to be held in Jamaica in May) and East Zone (to be staged in Thailand in September) will each offer four places in the final line-up.

Defending champions will be the USA, for whom the 'unbeatable' Fred Couples and Davis Love III won an unprecedented third consecutive title together last year in Puerto Rico. One wonders just what they have in store next, after their scintillating display at Dorado Beach, where, with all their rounds in the 60s, they shattered the previous best aggregate of 544 by eight strokes and equalled the biggest ever winning margin of 14 strokes. They now

Kingston Heath's magnificent bunkering will be on show when the Heineken Australian Open returns to Melbourne in late November

have Arnold Palmer and Jack Nicklaus' record four wins as a partnership (achieved in five years between 1963-67) firmly within their sights. Zimbabwe are not amongst the roll of past winning nations (led by the United States, who have now won exactly half of the 40 events), but the runners-up from the last two years will be hoping it will be third time lucky in 1995.

The Heineken World Cup is, of course, two events in one, with individual honours (in the form of the International Trophy) also at stake and last year proved third time lucky in this respect for Fred Couples. After finishing joint third in 1992 and second in 1993, he finally claimed the cherished prize (with a record 265 aggregate) in 1994, joining a long list of players who have completed the team and individual double in the same year. He will now be hoping to join the elite group of six multiple champions, led by Jack Nicklaus, record three-time winner and the only man to successfully defend the title.

Robert Allenby had looked a potential winner at The Vines last year, before a two-stroke penalty at the 10th in the final round proved ruinous. However, the tall Aussie eventually tasted Heineken success in 1994 when he claimed the 'major' of the southern hemisphere, the Heineken Australian Open, despite an inglorious finish at Royal Sydney, after carding four rounds of 70 for a 280 (eight under par) aggregate. Allenby, the 20th consecutive Australian or American to win his country's national title, will this year hope to become the first player, since six-time champion Jack Nicklaus, in 1976, to successfully defend the coveted Stonehaven Cup.

The Australian Open has a long and colourful history dating back to 1904 and this November the celebrated Kingston Heath Golf Club provides a fitting setting for the 80th championship. This classic test of golf, one of the great courses of the famous Melbourne sand belt, boasts bunkering by Dr Alister Mackenzie, who was so influential at its illustrious

neighbour, Royal Melbourne (as well as, of course, Augusta National and Cypress Point). Kingston Heath staged its first Australian Open in 1948 when four-time champion Ossie Pickworth notched his record third consecutive post war victory in the event. In 1957 Frank Phillips won the first of his two titles here, while in 1970 Gary Player recorded the sixth of his record seven successes. The club's fifth and last Open in 1989, saw a seven stroke victory for Peter Senior over Peter Fowler, champion at the course in 1983.

From Perth in February to Melbourne in November, Heineken's 1995 schedule, which takes in three continents, is one 'World Tour' that is bound to be well received by all, providing, as it does, four tournaments that any of the world's top golfers would be proud to win.

1995 HEINEKEN WORLD OF GOLF DATES
Feb 2 - 5   Heineken Classic
July 27 - 30   Heineken Dutch Open
Nov 9 - 12   Heineken World Cup Golf
Nov 23 - 26   Heineken Australian Open

The reigning Heineken Australian Open champion, Robert Allenby poses with the Stonehaven Cup

6

GREAT GOLF COURSES
OF THE WORLD

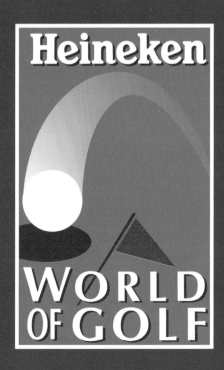

GREAT GOLF COURSES
OF THE WORLD

Golf, not only takes us, as Henry Longhurst used to say, to such beautiful places but it also guides us to a variety of extraordinary settings: from the glory of the West Virginia fall at The Greenbrier (previous pages) to the exotic, lush surrounds of the Blue Canyon Country Club in Phuket, Thailand (opposite). There are courses that cut into the side of foothills, as in Hakone, Japan (lower left), others, like Coolum on Queensland's Sunshine Coast (centre) that nestle in the shadow of mountains. Sometimes golfers must confront incredible hazards, as at the Lost City Golf Club in South Africa but afterwards they may retreat to the varied comforts of the nineteenth hole. (Lower right, the clubhouse at the Emirates Golf Club, Dubai)

(Opposite page) The Sunningdales and Walton Heaths of the 21st century perhaps? Three of southern England's newest and most highly acclaimed inland developments are Chart Hills (main picture) designed by Nick Faldo and Steve Smyers, The London Golf Club, a Jack Nicklaus creation and Hanbury Manor, the handiwork of his son, Jack Nicklaus Jr

Much more the work of Mother Nature than any man, among Britain's finest and most natural links courses are North Berwick in Scotland (top), Hoylake in England (centre) and The Island near Dublin

(Left) Playing
to the gallery:
the natural
amphitheatre
green on the
18th hole
at the
Olympic Club,
San Francisco
provides one
of golf's
greatest
stages

From the desert to the coast: contrasting images
of golf in America's Golden State. (Above) The 9th hole on
the Mountain Course at La Quinta and (below) the 16th
at Pelican Hill Golf Cub, Newport Coast, California